# PRACTICE PAPERS FOR

# CXC (CSEC) SPANISH

### PAULETTE A. RAMSAY
### ANNE MARIA BANKAY

LMH

Illustrations and images: Reproduced with permission from Microsoft Corporation.

Cover Design:  Sanya Dockery

Typesetting by:  Wayne Ho Sang Printing Services Ltd., Kingston 5. & Sanya Dockery

Published by: LMH Publishing Limited
7 Norman Road,
LOJ Industrial Complex
Building 10
Kingston C.S.O., Jamaica
Tel: 876-938-0005; 938-0712
Fax: 876-928-8038
Email: lmhpublishing@cwjamaica.com

Printed and bound by Lightning Source Inc., USA                    ISBN: 978-976-8202-66-6

# FOREWORD

Practice Papers for CXC Spanish is an essential text for students sitting CXC CSEC Spanish exam. It provides them with adequate practice exercises for the revised syllabus. Students may use the text independently or with the guidance of their teacher. This text is a prerequisite for students and teachers who desire success in CXC Spanish. ¡Aprovéchese de este texto!

**Errol Haughton**
*Past President, National Spanish Teachers' Association of Jamaica.*

"Por fin"a text in answer to such concerns as, 'What is this new CXC (CSEC) syllabus?', and 'How does one prepare for examination?' This book is certainly the reliable companion of teachers and students who will face the challenges of the CXC Examination with confidence and ultimately with success. The practice papers are extensive and well thought out with a variety of themes that should capture any student's interest. This text will undoubtedly be well received by teachers of Spanish. ¡Adelante!

**Ouida Lodge-Jones**
*Former President - Spanish Teachers' Association of Jamaica*

# ACKNOWLEDGEMENTS

The authors would like to thank Miss Mariana González
and Mrs. Aracelis Anedu for their help with proof-reading.
Special thanks to Miss Althea Aikens for typing.  Thanks
also to José Francisco Avila of Garífuna World Inc. for
permission to use information on the Garífuna culture.

# CONTENTS

**Listening Comprehension**
Preliminary Exercises and General Proficiency      1

**Directed Writing**
General Proficiency      43

**Letter/Compositions**
General Proficiency      57

**Contextual Announcements/Contextual Dialogues**
General Proficiency      65

**Reading Comprehension**
General Proficiency      83

**Reading Comprehension**
Additional Exercises      99

# LISTENING COMPREHENSION

## PRELIMINARY EXERCISES AND GENERAL PROFICIENCY

Candidates are required to select responses (multiple choice) to questions based on a continuous passage read in Spanish.

Questions and multiple choice answers are in English.
This section corresponds to **Paper I Section 4 and is worth 20 marks**.

# MIGUEL GOES TO CAMP

## PRELIMINARY EXERCISES

### Part A

1.  What was Miguel looking forward to next weekend?

    A.  His first camp.
    B.  Buying his new knapsack.
    C.  Buying his new sleeping bag.
    D.  His first free weekend.

2.  What did his mother purchase for him?

    A.  A knapsack.
    B.  A sleeping bag.
    C.  A notebook.
    D.  A pair of pajamas.

3.  What could he not wait to do?

    A.  Use his knapsack.
    B.  Use his list.
    C.  Use the articles in his bag.
    D.  Use his sleeping bag.

4.  Who made a check-list for Miguel?

    A.  His father.
    B.  His mother.
    C.  His parents.
    D.  His teacher.

5.     What did Miguel do when he realized it was raining?

   A.   He went back to bed.
   B.   He applauded.
   C.   He screamed.
   D.   He laughed.

6.     What did Miguel's father offer to do?

   A.   Telephone the teacher.
   B.   Telephone Miguel's friends.
   C.   Take him to the camp.
   D.   Take him to school.

7.     Who answered the telephone?

   A.   Miguel.
   B.   Miguel's father.
   C.   Miguel's mother.
   D.   Miguel's teacher.

8.     Why did Miguel applaud?

   A.   He was happy to see his parents.
   B.   He was happy that the rain had stopped.
   C.   He could still go to camp.
   D.   He was happy to see his teacher.

# MIGUEL GOES TO CAMP

## GENERAL PROFICIENCY

## Part A

1.    Why was Miguel excited?

    A.    He was going to leave home for the first time.

    B.    He was going to be with his friends.

    C.    He was going to his first camp that weekend.

    D.    He was going to buy his first knapsack.


2.    What did he do every night?

    A.    Check to see what his mother had bought him.

    B.    Check his list to see if he had everything.

    C.    Check to see if everything was in the knapsack.

    D.    Check to see if his knapsack was still there.


3.    What did he begin to use?

    A.    His sleeping bag.

    B.    His checklist.

    C.    His knapsack.

    D.    His money.


4.    Why did Miguel go to bed early on Thursday night?

    A.    So he would wake up early on Friday morning.

    B.    So that he would sleep well.

    C.    Because he was going to see his teacher on Friday.

    D.    Because he was tired.

# Part B

5.    What did Miguel realize when he awoke?

    A.   He was late.

    B.   He was not yet packed.

    C.   It was raining heavily.

    D.   It was drizzling.


6.    Why did his parents run to his room?

    A.   They had heard his knocks.

    B.   They had heard his coughs.

    C.   They had heard his screams

    D.   They had seen the rain.


7.    What happened while they were in Miguel's bedroom?

    A.   His teacher came to their house.

    B.   The telephone rang.

    C.   The rain stopped.

    D.   His father telephoned the teacher.


8.    What did the teacher tell Miguel's father?

    A.   To keep Miguel at home.

    B.   To give Miguel his regards.

    C.   To say that the camp was cancelled.

    D.   To say that the camp would still be held.

# ADOLFO'S BOOK

## PRELIMINARY EXERCISES

## Part A

1.    Which teacher recommended a book to the class?

    A.    The literature teacher.

    B.    The Cuban teacher.

    C.    The anthology teacher.

    D.    The history teacher.


2.    Why did Adolfo go to the bookstore?

    A.    To meet his friend.

    B.    To see if he could find the book.

    C.    To read the book.

    D.    To speak to the owner of the store.


3.    When did he go to the shopping centre?

    A.    Next day.

    B.    On Friday.

    C.    After class.

    D.    Before class.


4.    What happened at the store in the shopping centre?

    A.    Adolfo bought the book.

    B.    Adolfo could not afford the price of the book.

    C.    Adolfo did not like the book.

    D.    Adolfo did not find the book.

# Part B

5.  What did he decide to do when he returned home?

    A.  Show the book to his mother.
    B.  Show the book to his father.
    C.  Show the book to his brother.
    D.  Show the book to his sister.


6.  What did he do when he did not find the book?

    A.  He went back to the store.
    B.  He started to cry.
    C.  He telephoned the bookstore.
    D.  He called his mother.


7.  Who took him back to the bookstore?

    A.  His parents.
    B.  His brother.
    C.  His sister.
    D.  His mother.


8.  Who gave him his book at the bookstore?

    A.  His friend.
    B.  The owner of the store.
    C.  His mother.
    D.  The clerk in the store.

# ADOLFO'S BOOK

## GENERAL PROFICIENCY

## Part A

1. What did the teacher tell the class?

   A. To read a book.
   B. To buy a literature book.
   C. To buy a collection of Cuban accounts.
   D. To buy a collection of Cuban stories.

2. Where did Adolfo go?

   A. To a bookstore at his school.
   B. To a bookstore near his school.
   C. To a bookstore near his house.
   D. To a bookstore in the shopping centre.

3. Why did he not buy the book he found there?

   A. It was too expensive.
   B. It was not the one he wanted.
   C. It was in a bad condition.
   D. It was not for sale.

4. What did he decide to do next?

   A. Go to a bookstore in the.shopping centre.
   B. Go to the bookstore beside his house.
   C. Go to the library to look for the book.
   D. Go to a different shopping centre.

5.    What happened when Adolfo opened his bag?

    A.    He could not find the book.

    B.    He could not find his money.

    C.    He saw that his bag was empty.

    D.    He saw that his book was there.


6.    What did the manager tell him when he telephoned him?

    A.    That he had not found his book.

    B.    That he had found his book.

    C.    That he had sold his book.

    D.    That he had sent his book to him.


7.    What did the manager tell Adolfo when he arrived at the store?

    A.    That he could not find the book.

    B.    That he was too busy to talk to him.

    C.    That he did not remember speaking to him.

    D.    That he had sent the book to him.


8.    Why did Adolfo hug the store clerk?

    A.    Because he knew who he was.

    B.    Because he was happy to see him.

    C.    Because he gave him his book.

    D.    Because he bought the book for him.

# ENRIQUE'S NIGHTMARE

## PRELIMINARY EXERCISES

### Part A

1.  What did Enrique sec when he opened his eyes?

    A.  Three strange objects in the room.
    B.  Three persons in the room.
    C.  Three round objects in the room.
    D.  Three identical objects in the room.

2.  What did he see to the right of the room?

    A.  A vase with flowers and some cards.
    B.  A table with flowers and some cards.
    C.  A television and two armchairs.
    D.  A television, an armchair and two small chairs.

3.  What did he think when he could not get up?

    A.  That he was tied to the bed.
    B.  That he was badly hurt.
    C.  That he was very ill.
    D.  That he was in the hospital.

4.  What did he do when he could not get up?

    A.  He shouted to the nurse.
    B.  He began to scream.
    C.  He began to cry.
    D.  He shouted for his mother.

# Part B

5.    Who heard Enrique's screams?

   A.    His mother.
   B.    His parents.
   C.    The nurses.
   D.    The nurse and doctor.

6.    What did Enrique do when he got out of bed?

   A.    He discussed his problem with his mother.
   B.    He bathed and got dressed.
   C.    He had breakfast and then got dressed.
   D.    He bathed and had breakfast.

7.    What was he going to do with his fliends?

   A.    Buy a new toy bicycle.
   B.    Buy a new bicycle.
   C.    Have a bicycle race.
   D.    Have a bicycle sale with them.

8.    Who was taking Enrique to the hospital?

   A.    The rider of the bicycle with which he collided.
   B.    His mother and his fiends.
   C.    His friends and their parents.
   D.    The driver of the car with which he collided.

# ENRIQUE'S NIGHTMARE

## GENERAL PROFICIENCY

## Part A

1.      What happened when Enrique opened his eyes?

   A.   He could not see.

   B.   He did not recognize the room.

   C.   He was frightened.

   D.   He became very ill.

2.      What did he see to the left of the room?

   A.   A vase with flowers and some cards.

   B.   A television and two small chairs.

   C.   A table with flowers and some cards.

   D.   A television and an armchair.

3.      What happened when he tried to get up?

   A.   He could not do so.

   B.   He fell out of bed.

   C.   He hurt himself badly.

   D.   He did it very easily.

4.      Why did he begin to scream?

   A.   He heard a frightening sound.

   B.   He realized he was in the hospital.

   C.   He heard the nurse's voice.

   D.   He thought he was in hospital.

# Part B

5.     How did Enrique realize that he was dreaming?

    A.    His mother awoke him and told him.

    B.    He fell out of the chair.

    C.    He saw himself in the mirror.

    D.    He was very afraid.

6.     What did he do after he bathed and got dressed?

    A.    He went to the kitchen and hurriedly had breakfast.

    B.    He went to the kitchen and prepared breakfast.

    C.    He went to the kitchen and helped his mother.

    D.    He went to the kitchen and told his mother to hurry.

7.     What happened when he raced on to the street?

    A.    He hit a chauffeur.

    B.    He collided with a car.

    C.    He made a sudden turn.

    D.    He fell off the bicycle.

8.     Whal did the driver do?

    A.    Put Enrique back on his bicycle.

    B.    Called his friends immediately.

    C.    Put him in his car and took him to the hospital.

    D.    Called his mother immediately.

# A DAY IN THE PARK

## PRELIMINARY EXERCISES

### Part A

1.    Who did Rosario telephone?

    A.   Her friend Carmen.

    B.   Her father's friend.

    C.   Her mother's friend.

    D.   Her sister's friend.

2.    What was being celebrated?

    A.   Rosario's birthday.

    B.   Rosario's father's birthday.

    C.   Rosario's mother's birthday.

    D.   Rosario's friend's birthday.

3.    Who wanted to play baseball?

    A.   Rosario and Carmen.

    B.   Rosario's father.

    C.   Rosario's mother.

    D.   Rosario's sister.

4.    How many candles did Rosario put on the cake.

    A.   Twenty.

    B.   Thirty.

    C.   Forty.

    D.   Twenty-five.

5.    Where did they take a walk after lunch?

    A.    In the garden.

    B.    In the picnic area.

    C.    In the shade.

    D.    In the pastures.

6.    How were they feeling when they decided to leave?

    A.    They were feeling happy.

    B.    They were feeling tired.

    C.    They were feeling hungry.

    D.    They were feeling sad.

7.    What were they looking for under the tree?

    A.    Their basket.

    B.    Their clothes.

    C.    Their books.

    D.    Their flowers.

8.    How did they find it?

    A.    A man gave it to them.

    B.    Rosario saw it in the tree.

    C.    A lady gave it to them.

    D.    Rosario's father saw it in the tree.

# A DAY IN THE PARK

## GENERAL PROFICIENCY

## Part A

1.  What did Rosario invite Carmen to do?

    A.  Go to her house.
    B.  Go on a picnic with her.
    C.  Go to a party with her.
    D.  Go to see her mother with her.

2.  What did Rosario's father want to do?

    A.  He wanted to eat.
    B.  He wanted to rest.
    C.  He wanted to play baseball.
    D.  He wanted to take a walk.

3.  What did they have to eat?

    A.  Sandwiches, chicken, fruit and cake.
    B.  Sandwiches, cake, wine and chicken.
    C.  Chicken, fruit, cake, wine and sandwiches.
    D.  Chicken, cake, wine and fruit.

4.  What happened after Rosario put the candles on the cake?

    A.  She could not find the matches.
    B.  She lit them.
    C.  She hugged her mother.
    D.  She cut the cake.

# Part B

5.     What did they do after they ate?

     A.    They picked some flowers in the garden.

     B.    They went for a walk in the garden.

     C.    They played "pass the ball" in the garden.

     D.    They passed by the garden.

6.     What happened when they decided to go home?

     A.    They could not find their basket.

     B.    They could not find Rosario.

     C.    They could not find their way out.

     D.    They could not find their favourite tree.

7.     What did they hear when they decided to leave?

     A.    The voice of a woman.

     B.    The voice of a baby.

     C.    The voice of Rosario.

     D.    The voice of a man.

8.     What did this person tell them?

     A.    That they should leave immediately.

     B.    That they should not leave.

     C.    That he had their basket.

     D.    That they had his basket.

# ISABEL'S SURPRISE

## PRELIMINARY EXERCISES

## Part A

1.    With whom did Isabel go to the beauty salon?

    A.    With her friend.

    B.    With her mother.

    C.    With her sister.

    D.    With her teacher.


2.    Why did they go to the beauty salon?

    A.    They wanted to talk to the owner.

    B.    They wanted to look pretty for a concert.

    C.    They wanted to see the other clients.

    D.    They wanted to see the inside of the beauty salon.


3.    What did they want to do?

    A.    Cut their hair.

    B.    Paint their nails.

    C.    Cut their hair and paint their nails.

    D.    Cut their hair and nails.


4.    What did the hairdresser say they would have to do?

    A.    Wait.

    B.    Leave.

    C.    Cut off their hair.

    D.    Cut their nails.

5.      Why did they decide to leave the salon?

    A.    It was very late.

    B.    It was too crowded.

    C.    They did not like the hairdresser.

    D.    They did not like the salon.


6.      What did they leave for the hairdresser?

    A.    A note explaining why they had to leave.

    B.    Money for her services.

    C.    A note saying goodbye.

    D.    Some information for clients.


7.      Why did they take a taxi?

    A.    They had missed the bus.

    B.    They did not like the bus.

    C.    They did not like the salon.

    D.    They had missed the hairdresser.


8.      Where did they go?

    A.    To Marta's house.

    B.    To Isabel's house.

    C.    To the concert.

    D.    To look for the hairdresser.

# ISABEL'S SURPRISE

## GENERAL PROFICIENCY

## Part A

1.     Where did Isabel and Marta go?

    A.    To Marta's house.

    B.    To a beauty salon.

    C.    To a concert.

    D.    To an elegant store.

2.     What were they going to do after that?

    A.    Go to a party.

    B.    Go to a concert.

    C.    Visit their friend.

    D.    Visit their clients.

3.     When would the hairdresser attend to them?

    A.    In five minutes' time.

    B.    In an hour's time.

    C.    When she had combed her hair.

    D.    When she was finished with the other clients.

4.     What did the girls decide to do?

    A.    Wait.

    B.    Leave.

    C.    Call their parents.

    D.    Call their friends.

# Part B

5.    Why did they call their parents?

    A.    To ask their permission to go to a party.

    B.    To ask their permission to change their hairstyles.

    C.    To let them know where they were.

    D.    To let them speak to the hairdresser.

6.    What happened to them while they waited?

    A.    They became nervous and anxious.

    B.    They became tired.

    C.    They beeame anxious.

    D.    They became anxious and tired.

7.    How long did they wait?

    A.    One hour.

    B.    Two hours.

    C.    More than two and a half hours.

    D.    Half an hour.

8.    What did they discover at Isabel's house?

    A.    That the night of the concert had passed.

    B.    That they were mistaken about the date of the concert.

    C.    That they were too late for the eoncert.

    D.    That the concert would be on Thursday night.

# A LATE ARRIVAL

## PRELIMINARY EXERCISES

## Part A

I. When the alarm clock sounded the narrator...

    A.   jumped out of bed.

    B.   went back to sleep.

    C.   was sweating and trembling.

    D.   covered his head with the sheet.

2. What did the narrator feel like doing?

    A.   Going back to sleep.

    B.   Jumping out of bed.

    C.   Going into his mother's bedroom.

    D.   Putting the sheet on the bed.

3. Why did the narrator have to get up right away?

    A.   His mother wanted to spread the bed.

    B.   His breakfast was ready.

    C.   He would be late.

    D.   He had to go into his mother's room.

4. Why did the narrator run from the house?

    A.   The bus he wanted had left him.

    B.   His mother told him to run as it was 6 o'clock.

    C.   He had spent too much time eating breakfast.

    D.   He wanted to catch the 6 o'clock bus.

5.    How long was the bus ride?

      A.    Many hours.

      B.    One hour.

      C.    Fifty minutes.

      D.    One hour and a quarter.

6.    Why did the narrator start running?

      A.    He wanted to arrive on time.

      B.    He wanted to run for a long distance.

      C.    He did not want the bus to disappear.

      D.    He wanted to get to the bus.

7.    The narrator did not know the time because...

      A.    he had left his watch on the bus.

      B.    he had forgotten his watch at home.

      C.    his watch had stopped working.

      D.    he was always unfortunate with his watch.

8.    What did the narrator do when he reached his destination?

      A.    He asked what time it was.

      B.    He asked what he should do.

      C.    He apologised for arriving late.

      D.    He asked for the boss.

# A LATE ARRIVAL

## GENERAL PROFICIENCY

## Part A

1. How did the narrator get awake?

    A. His mother woke him.

    B. He heard a strange sound.

    C. The alarm clock rang.

    D. The bed was shaking.

2. The narrator's mother told him that...

    A. he could sleep for a few minutes more.

    B. he would have to run very fast.

    C. he had to leave the house immediately.

    D. he would be late and should get up immediately.

3. The narrator's mother...

    A. prepared his breakfast.

    B. covered him with the sheet.

    C. ran outside to stop the bus.

    D. went to her bedroom.

4. What did the narrator have for breakfast?

    A. Ham and eggs.

    B. Eggs and bread.

    C. Bread and jam.

    D. Ham and bread.

5.      What did the narrator realise when he got off the bus?

        A.   That he had arrived late.

        B.   That he was on the wrong street.

        C.   That he had a long distance to walk.

        D.   That he had taken the wrong bus.


6.      The narrator did not know. . .

        A.   what time it was.

        B.   where he was going.

        C.   how long he should wait.

        D.   where he had left his watch.


7.      When the boss arrived, what did he say to the narrator?

        A.   He asked why the narrator arrived late.

        B.   He apologised for arriving late.

        C.   He asked what time the narrator had arrived.

        D.   He gave an excuse for his late arrival.


8.      After speaking to the narrator, the boss...

        A.   told him to start working.

        B.   introduced the narrator to the other employees.

        C.   told the employees about the late arrival.

        D.   went away for an hour and a half.

# A VALUABLE LESSON

## PRELIMINARY EXERCISES

### Part A

1.      Where was the narrator born?

   A.   In a small town.

   B.   In Kingston.

   C.   Near the primary school.

   D.   On a farm.


2.      The narrator did not go to secondary school because...

   A.   his brothers and sisters had to go.

   B.   his parents could not afford it.

   C.   he had to sell vegetables.

   D.   he was living in Kingston.


3.      What did the children do on the farm?

   A.   They did their school work.

   B.   They set up a big market.

   C.   They had a good time.

   D.   They planted vegetables.


4.      The narrator's mother. . .

   A.   went to Kingston to live.

   B.   cultivated vegetables on the farm.

   C.   went to market to sell vegetables.

   D.   took vegetables to the secondary school.

5.      What did the narrator do in the market?

    A.      He bought vegetables from a man.

    B.      He helped his mother to sell.

    C.      He marked the price of the vegetables.

    D.      He spent time speaking to the buyers.


6.      What did the narrator learn after some years had passed?

    A.      To dress and speak well.

    B.      That it was important to arrive on time.

    C.      What he had to do to graduate.

    D.      That too many years had passed for him to graduate.


7.      What had happened to the narrator's family after some years?

    A.      They also moved to Kingston.

    B.      Life had improved for them.

    C.      They still lived in the country.

    D.      They moved to a better town.


8.      What lesson did the narrator learn?

    A.      That money was very important.

    B.      That his parents should be invited to the activities.

    C.      That he was really proud of his family.

    D.      That he would receive a present.

# A VALUABLE LESSON

## GENERAL PROFICIENCY

## Part A

1.      The narrator was born...

       A.   in Kingston.

       B.   near the primary school.

       C.   on a farm.

       D.   in a small town.

Why could the narrator go only to primary school?

       A.   The secondary school was too far.

       B.   His parents had enough money so he did not have to save more.

       C.   His parents felt that secondary education was unnecessary.

       D.   His parents could not afford to send him.

3.      The children had to...

       A.   do their school work.

       B.   go to market.

       C.   work and plant vegetables.

       D.   sell vegetables.

4.      Why did the narrator's mother go to Kingston?

       A.   To live there.

       B.   To sell vegetables.

       C.   To cultivate vegetables.

       D.   To take the narrator to school.

5.     The man who bought vegetables from the narrator's mother offered to...

    A.   buy more vegetables.

    B.   take the mother to meet his family.

    C.   pay for the narrator's secondary education.

    D.   take them back to the country.

6.     Where would the narrator live?

    A.   In an academic institution.

    B.   With the man's family.

    C.   With his parents.

    D.   At the secondary school.

7.     The narrator did not want to invite his parents to his graduation because...

    A.   they lived far away in the country.

    B.   he believed his parents did not have the money to come to Kingston.

    C.   he thought his friends would not accept his parents.

    D.   he thought his friends would reject him once they met his parents.

8.     What happened after the graduation?

    A.   There were many activities.

    B.   Many presentations were made.

    C.   The narrator was congratulated by his parents.

    D.   The narrator's father wished him a Merry Christmas.

# A DISAPPOINTING TRIP

## PRELIMINARY EXERCISES

### Part A

I.  Where were the students going?

    A.  To a camp.

    B.  To the San Martin School.

    C.  To meet some young people.

    D.  To the country.

2.  The students were going to...

    A.  prepare a meal.

    B.  learn some Geography from the teacher.

    C.  climb a mountain.

    D.  study a map of the region.

3.  Why was the teacher a good guide?

    A.  She knew the place and had climbed that mountain.

    B.  She had gone on excursions many times.

    C.  She was well-known in the area.

    D.  She liked excursions.

4.  What did the teacher realize?

    A.  That she had not counted the students.

    B.  That everything was all right.

    C.  That a student was missing.

    D.  That some students were falling behind.

## Part B

5. What did they hear in the bushes?

   A. A roaring sound.

   B. Singing.

   C. Crying.

   D. A loud noise.

6. What had 'happened?

   A. A boy had run away.

   B. A boy had hurt himself.

   C. A stone had fallen on the boy.

   D. The boy had tried to walk too far.

7. When the boy called out...

   A. his companions came.

   B. the teacher came.

   C. nobody replied.

   D. he felt more pain.

8. Where was the boy taken by his friends?

   A. To the top of the mountain.

   B. To a place where he could lie down.

   C. To the foot of the mountain.

   D. To the hospital.

# A DISAPPOINTING TRIP

## GENERAL PROFICIENCY

## Part A

I.      When the students set out they felt...

   A.   that it was too early.

   B.   very excited.

   C.   that the mountain was too high.

   D.   that they should have left at 5 o'clock.


2.      Why did the Geography teacher go with the students?

   A.   She had a good map of the area.

   B.   It was a Geography trip.

   C.   She liked to go on trips.

   D.   She liked the food they were taking.


3.      The Geography teacher was going as a guide because she...

   A.   always enjoyed excursions.

   B.   had climbed various mountains.

   C.   knew the place and had climbed that mountain.

   D.   was from that area.


4.      When the student was discovered missing, the teacher. . .

   A.   decided to return home immediately.

   B.   sent the students ahead.

   C.   tried to find out what had happened.

   D.   decided to search for him.

# Part B

5.        What did the students discover in the bushes?

        A.    That the boy was getting attention.

        B.    That the boy was still crying.

        C.    That the missing boy was there.

        D.    That the boy had been searching for something.

6.        Where did the boy feel pain?

        A.    In the area under his shirt.

        B.    In his back.

        C.    In his leg and head.

        D.    In his right leg.

7.        What was the result of the fall?

        A.    The boy's leg was cut.

        B.    The boy could only walk a short distance.

        C.    The boy's shirt was torn.

        D.    The boy became unconscious.

8.        What did the boy try to do but could not?

        A.    Reply to the shouts he heard.

        B.    Call out to someone.

        C.    Get up and walk.

        D.    Look for his friends.

# A SURPRISING MOVIE

## PRELIMINARY EXERCISES

### Part A

I.  When did the narrator go to bed?

    A.   At about 8 o'clock.

    B.   At 6 o'clock.

    C.   At 10 o'clock.

    D.   At midnight.

2.  What did the narrator do until late?

    A.   He went to the movies.

    B.   He looked at a film at home.

    C.   He went shopping with his father.

    D.   He visited another little boy.

3.  What happened to the little boy in the movie?

    A.   He got lost while shopping with his father.

    B.   He went to see his father.

    C.   He bought something for his father.

    D.   He went visiting with his father.

4.  Why did the little boy leave his father?

    A.   He wanted to speak to a guard.

    B.   He wanted to play with a friend.

    C.   He wanted to find the Toy Department.

    D.   He wanted to get some help.

## Part B

5.     Why was the father frantic?

    A.    Because the boy was playing with toys.

    B.    Because he wanted to see a movie.

    C.    Because he could not find his son.

    D.    Because the guard did not help him.

6.     What did the boy do in the cafeteria?

    A.    He bought cakes and sandwiches.

    B.    He ate cakes and then paid for them.

    C.    He did not pay for what he ate.

    D.    He asked a guard to pay for the cakes.

7.     How did the father find out what had happened?

    A.    He saw his son and spoke to him.

    B.    He asked the lady in the cafeteria.

    C.    He asked the guard.

    D.    The people in the Toy Department told him.

8.     What happened two years before?

    A.    The narrator and his father had an accident.

    B.    The narrator left his father in a store.

    C.    The narrator had an experience similar to the one in the movie.

    D.    The narrator celebrated his second birthday.

# A SURPRISING MOVIE

## GENERAL PROFICIENCY

### Part A

I.    Why was the narrator awake until late?

    A.   He was eight years old on that day.

    B.   His friend was visiting him.

    C.   He looked at a movie.

    D.   He went out with his father.

2.    The father went shopping and...

    A.   bought a tie.

    B.   selected some toys.

    C.   chose a suit and some ties.

    D.   bought some clothes.

3.    What did the little boy do while his father was shopping?

    A.   He left the store.

    B.   He waited for 2 hours.

    C.   He went to the Toy Department.

    D.   He went to look for a guard.

4.    Why did the father need help?

    A.   He had a problem with the guards.

    B.   He could not find his son.

    C.   He could not decide what to buy.

    D.   He could not find the Toy Department.

5.      The little boy was having a good time because...

     A.   he was with his father.

     B.   he was playing with toys.

     C.   his father bought him a remote control car.

     D.   he went for a train ride.


6.      What did the guard in the cafeteria do?

     A.   He paid for the food the boy ate.

     B.   He put the boy outside.

     C.   He took the boy to his father.

     D.   He took the boy to the Toy Department.


7.      What did the father ask the guard?

     A.   If he knew what had happened.

     B.   If his son was in the cafeteria.

     C.   If he had seen his son.

     D.   If his son had bought food in the cafeteria,


8.      Why was the movie surprising to the narrator?

     A.   His father looked like the father in the movie.

     B.   The end was not what he expected.

     C.   He had a big surprise when he went shopping.

     D.   The same thing had happened to him.

# THE MISSING BAG

## PRELIMINARY EXERCISES

### Part A

1.  The eight people had been friends since they. ..

    A.  first met in a restaurant.
    B.  became successful.
    C.  established their business.
    D.  were in primary school.

2.  Why were the friends meeting?

    A.  They were celebrating their success.
    B.  They wanted to start a business together.
    C.  They had just graduated from primary school.
    D.  They always laughed when they were together.

3.  What did Marta suddenly say to her friends?

    A.  That she was sorry she had come.
    B.  That she had found a lot of money.
    C.  That she could not find her bag.

That she had counted the money.

4.  Where was Marta's money?

    A.  She had left it at home.
    B.  It was in the bag.
    C.  She had given it to a friend.
    D.  She had used it to pay the bill.

# Part B

5.      What did Marta ask her friends to do?

     A.    Pay for another bag.

     B.    Leave the restaurant.

     C.    Give her some money.

     D.    Help her to look for the bag.

6.      Why were Marta's friends upset?

     A.    Because she was crying.

     B.    Because they could not get to eat.

     C.    Because they wanted to talk.

     D.    Because they could not find her anywhere.

7.      What had happened to Marta's bag?

     A.    She had brought it to the restaurant.

     B.    She had given it to a man to keep for her.

     C.    She had left it in a taxi.

     D.    She had put it on her seat.

8.      Why did Marta give the man money?

     A.    She had forgotten to pay her taxi fare.

     B.    She wanted to reward him for being honest.

     C.    She owed him $500.

     D.    She was pleased with the ride in the taxi.

# THE MISSING BAG

## GENERAL PROFICIENCY

## Part A

1.    When did the friends meet each other for the first time?

    A.    When they set up a business together.

    B.    When they were in a restaurant.

    C.    When they became successful.

    D.    When they were in primary school.

2.    The reason for the meeting was that the friends...

    A.    were hungry and wanted to eat.

    B.    had just left school.

    C.    wanted to have a good time together.

    D.    planned to set up a business together.

3.    Marta was very sure that…

    A.    she had entered the restaurant on time.

    B.    the restaurant was good.

    C.    the bag was left in the restaurant.

    D.    she had the bag when she entered the restaurant.

4.    What was Marta wondering?

    A.    If she should ask the waiter about the bag.

    B.    If her camera was in the bag.

    C.    If the bag had been stolen.

    D.    If her friends would question her about the bag.

5.    Marta asked her friends to ...

    A.    help her look for the bag.

    B.    give her some money.

    C.    pay for the meal.

    D.    pay for another bag.


6.    The man who came into the room said that...

    A.    the seat of his taxi had been damaged by a woman.

    B.    a woman who had taken his taxi had not paid him.

    C.    a woman had left a bag in his taxi.

    D.    trash had been left on the seat of his taxi.


7.    Why had the man come to the restaurant?

    A.    He discovered the damage to his car.

    B.    He thought the woman might need her bag.

    C.    He wanted to eat in that restaurant.

    D.    He wanted to find the woman as quickly as possible.


8.    What did Marta's friends do?

    A.    They explained to her that they had to leave.

    B.    They paid the bill of $500.

    C.    They left the restaurant without speaking to Marta.

    D.    They said goodbye to Marta and left without explaining why.

# DIRECTED WRITING

## GENERAL PROFICIENCY

This section corresponds to **Paper 2, Section 1 and is worth 30 marks**.

# DIRECTED WRITNG

## GENERAL PROFICIENCY

Write in SPANISH the information required by each of the situations given below. **Do not use more than one sentence for each situation**. DO NOT translate the situations given.

1.  You are leaving home on an exchange programme to a Spanish-speaking country. Write the note which your sister leaves on your bed with a suggestion for improving your Spanish.

2.  Your mother has written strict instructions about an electrical appliance which she recently bought. Write one of the instructions.

3.  A nurse at the hospital where you are visiting your sick friend allows you to see him but before doing so, she shows you the note of caution which was written by his doctor. Write the note.

4.  You have a part-time job but you cannot come to work this week. Write a message to your boss saying why you will be absent.

5.  You are in a restaurant waiting on a friend who is an hour late and you decide to leave. Write a message, which you leave with the waiter, apologising for not being there.

6.  While your parents are on vacation in Mexico you become involved in something that occupies a lot of your time. Write a message to your parents explaining why you cannot meet them at the airport.

7.  You were the victim of a robbery a week ago and the police need you to come to the station immediately to identify the robber. Write the note you leave for your parents explaining your absence.

8. Your parents told you to stay at home but you suddenly develop severe pains in your stomach and decide to seek help. Write a message to your parents saying where you have gone.

9. You go to your friend's house to discuss a matter with him but he has gone out. Leave a message for him telling him why you came by.

10. You have spent all your pocket money and want to go to the movies. Write a message to your brother requesting his assistance.

11. You have an evening job as a receptionist in a hotel and a gentleman phones to make a reservation. Write a message to the Supervisor explaining the arrangements you made.

12. You return home from school on your birthday and see a gift from your parents but you have arranged to go out with your friends. Write a message to your parents expressing your appreciation.

13. You want to cancel your arrangements to see your friend next week because something unexpected has occurred. Write a note of apology to him/her.

14. A passenger in front of you wants to know how the old lady next to him would react to his smoking but discovers that she is deaf. Write the note which he shows her in an effort to find this out.

15. You have decided to participate in an activity which is being planned by a club in your community but your mother is not in favour of this. Write the note which she leaves for you to warn you of the risk involved.

16. Your little cousin has been trying to complete a task for the past two weeks and telephones to ask for you while you are out. Write the message which your brother takes.

17. A girlfriend has just had her hair done. Write a message to her in class saying what you think of her new hairstyle.

18. You agreed to help a classmate with an assignment. Pass a note to your classmate giving a reason for changing your mind.

19. You have just received an unexpected invitation to a party but have nothing suitable to wear. Write a note in which you ask your sister, who will return home while you are out, to lend you a specific item of clothing.

20. Your father is giving a speech at his Company's Award Ceremony and the guests are falling asleep. Write a note to your father suggesting what he should do.

21. Your teacher has asked you to deliver a message to a student in another class but you understand that he has left the school. Leave a note for your teacher in which you provide her with his new address.

22. You have house guests for whom you leave a special instruction in the bathroom. Write the instruction.

23. You have not seen your mother and you are going to the airport. Write the good-bye note which you leave for her.

24. While your family is visiting friends, your brother is being impossible. Write the note in which you tell him what you expect of him.

25. You need to speak to your pastor but he is not in his office when you get there. Write a message in which you tell him what you want to talk to him about.

26. Your mother sends you with a note in which she apologises to her friend for not being able to meet her at the airport. Write the note.

27. Your father is unable to go to work and sends you to his colleague with a special request. Write the request.

28.      You are at a concert with your girlfriend who did not hear something that was said by the Master of Ceremonies. Write the note which she passes to you to query the statement.

29.      While you were out your brother wanted your opinion on something. Write the note which he leaves for you.

30.      Your friend passes you a note during class time asking you to explain a word. Write a note in which you tell her why you are not able to do so.

31.      Your aunt has had an accident. Write the note you send to convey your sympathy to her.

32.      Your cousin has just been successful in his exams. Write the congratulatory note which you send him.

33.      You are unable to attend classes and send an excuse to your teacher with a friend explaining the reason for your absence. Write the excuse.

34.      You are on vacation and arrive at a hotel to check in but there is no one at the desk to receive you. You leave your luggage and a note for the receptionist. Write the note.

35.      You have been awaiting the arrival of a friend but have to leave home suddenly. Write the note which you leave for him to explain your absence.

36.      Your parents expect you home at a certain time but you will be late. Write a note which you send with your sister to explain the reason you will not be home on time.

37.      Your aunt has sent you a lovely gift for your birthday. Write a note to thank her.

38.      You are giving a party at your home. Write the short invitation you email to your friends giving them information about the party.

39.    You go to your friend's house to tell her about your recent trip abroad but she is not there. Write the note you leave to describe your trip.

40.    While your mother is out, an old friend of hers stops by to see her. Write the note which she leaves with you expressing her disappointment.

41.    Your sister has an urgent problem and wants you to contact your mother at work. Write the text message you send to your mother at work, telling her what has happened to your sister.

42.    You and your classmate have different opinions as to which team will win a sporting event tomorrow. Write your classmate's prediction of the outcome of the event.

43.    You need a book from the nearby library but do not have time to get it, so you ask your brother to get it for you. Write the note which you give to him to take to the librarian requesting her help in finding the book.

44.    Your classmate is planning to visit your home. Write a note in which you tell him what time is convenient for him to do so.

45.    During a shopping trip you were assisted by a very friendly attendant. Write the note you send to her, expressing your appreciation.

46.    You go to your aunt's office to discuss a matter with her but she is not there. Write a note to her informing her that you had come and explaining why you wanted to see her.

47.    Your sister is going to visit your grandmother but you are unable to go. Write the message you send, telling her when you will visit.

48.    Your friends will be visiting your church for the first time. Write a note telling them where it is located.

49.    Your parents have decided to punish your little brother for something which he did at school, but you believe that the punishment is too harsh. Write a note to your parents expressing your disagreement with their decision.

50. Your brother has promised to visit your friend in Venezuela while he is travelling there. Write a note to your friend in which you introduce your brother to him/her.

51. You have recommended your dressmaker/tailor to your friend. Write a note to your dressmaker/tailor confirming that you recommended him/her.

52. You ask your sister to return something which you bought at a store and later discovered was damaged. Write a note which you give to her to take to the store.

53. The manager of the store where you have applied for a job sends a message to you concerning the outcome of your application. Write the message.

54. An exchange student at your school accepts your invitation to go to a place of interest but she has to go somewhere else first. Write the note she gives you to remind you of where to pick her up.

55. Your new neighbour asks you to attend his birthday party but you do not accept the invitation. Write the note you receive from him persuading you to attend.

56. You went to the flower shop to buy flowers for your grandmother for a special occasion. Write the message which you write to accompany the flowers.

57. Your friend has a tragedy in her family. Write a note in which you offer your sympathy.

58. You are not in agreement with something your sister has done. Write a note to her expressing your disapproval.

59. You want to avoid discussing a matter with your brother. Write a note to him expressing your disagreement with his views.

60. You doubt very much that your friend's involvement in a particular concert is a good idea. Write a note expressing your doubts to her.

61. You have just listened to a very controversial discussion between your brother and his friends. You do not want to become involved but you later leave him a note expressing your personal view on the matter. Write the note.

62. You have received an invitation to a function which you are unable to attend. Write a note in which you express your regrets.

63. Your friend has been kind enough to do a big favour for you. Write a note to thank him.

64. Your mother is visiting your aunt whom you have not seen in many years. Write a note to your aunt expressing your best wishes to her.

65. It is your father's birthday. Write a message to him expressing your good wishes.

66. A student who has been unfriendly to you in the past, sends you a note in class indicating a change of attitude. Write the note you receive.

67. Your younger brother has been very worried lately. Write the note he sends you asking for advice.

68. You want to miss a basketball match on Wednesday and send a message to the coach. Write the message he sends you telling you why you have to play.

69. Your friend's mother is ill and you send a note to her to express your wishes for a quick recovery. Write the note.

70. Your cousin in Trinidad has an important examination to sit. Write a note to express your hope that he/she will be successful.

71. Your parents have decided to punish you for taking the car without permission. Write a note to them to explain why you did this.

72. You would like the bookstore in town to order a special book for you. Write the note which you send to the manager.

73. You are thinking of doing a Summer Course abroad. Write a note to your teacher asking for advice on the matter.

74. You think your friend spends her money unwisely. Write a note to warn her about this matter.

75. Your friend is not speaking to you because she is upset that you have chosen the prettier of two things which you both bought. Write a note in which you compare both things favourably.

76. You learn that your friend who lives in Canada is in your country for a few days. He is not at his hotel when you go to see him. Write a note offering to take him to a place of interest.

77. You would like to get your mother's opinion on a matter but she is not at home and you have to leave. Write the note which you leave, requesting her opinion.

78. Your aunt has written to tell you to choose one of two things which she is thinking of buying for you. Write a note to her expressing your preference.

79. You decided not to be involved in any of the co-curricular activities in your school. Write the note you receive from the president of one of the clubs, telling you the advantages of joining her club.

80. Your teacher invites someone to address your class. During the address she sends a message to you telling you that she wants you to do something. Write the message you receive from your teacher.

81. While you are not at home a phone call comes for you from abroad. Write the message that your father leaves for you telling you what the caller said.

82. You feel very certain about a situation which your teacher is questioning. Write a note to her expressing this certainty.

83. You send a Christmas card to your sister who is abroad studying. Write the greetings which you send.

84. Your Spanish teacher has recently got married. Write a congratulatory note which you give to her in the Spanish class.

85. Your younger brother has a serious difficulty with a certain situation. Write a note in which you suggest a solution.

86. You have been invited to a special birthday celebration for your friend's father. Write the note of acceptance which you send to her mother.

87. A friend who has migrated writes you a letter. Write the first line of the reply you send to your friend, telling him/her how happy you were to receive his/her letter.

88. You have been grounded by your parents for failing to observe a family rule. Write a note apologising for your mistake.

89. You have been invited to a special function but need to have more information about it. Write a brief note to the organizers requesting information on two aspects of the function.

90. You have just returned from your cousin's home where you spent a week. Write a note in which you tell him/her what you enjoyed most about the visit.

91. You want your brother to do a favour for you. Write the note which you leave for him, promising him to return the favour.

92. You are at your best friend's house and his mother passes you a note requesting your help in planning a surprise party for your friend. Write the note.

93.    Your older brother does not want anyone to enter his room when he is not there. Write the notice he puts on his door explaining the reason for his position.

94.    A Venezuelan student has recently started attending your school. You receive a note from her requesting your help to improve her English. Write the note.

95.    Your friends invite you to go to the movies with them, but your parents are not at home to give you permission. Write the note which you leave for them, telling them when you will return.

96.    You spent a weekend with your friend in another town. Write a note to him/her telling him/her how you felt about the visit.

97.    Your friend is leaving to study abroad. Write a note which you give him at the airport wishing him success and best wishes.

98.    You were punished by your parents for being rude to one of their friends. Write a note to them telling them what lesson you learned from this.

99.    Your friend has just passed her CXC Spanish Examination. Write a brief note telling her how you think this will help in the future.

100.   Your mother is not at home when you return from school but she has left a note instructing you to do a special chore. Write the note.

101.   Your friend emails you to tell you that you offended her/him with something you said to her/him at school. Write your email response apologizing to your friend.

102.   Your favourite aunt who had promised to visit you during the summer has written to say she will not be able to keep her promise. Write a note to her expressing your disappointment.

103.   Your parents are away and you want to borrow something they have said you should never touch. Write an email to them requesting permission to use the item.

104. You are reluctant to buy an article for your brother. Write the note he leaves for you explaining the reason he needs the article.

105. Write a note to your friend expressing regret at her loss in a competition.

106. Your neighbour has been away for a long time and is returning soon. Write the note you place on his/her door to greet him/her.

107. You go to a particular section of the library to find material for a project. There is a notice on the door explaining a problem with that section. What does the notice say?

108. You have been waiting on your friend for more than an hour at the library, but need to leave. Write the note you leave for him/her giving directions to where you can be found.

109. You are very disappointed with your brother's attitude toward your friend. Write a note expressing this disappointment.

110. You have been away and your family is expecting you home but you have a change of plans. Write a note to them informing them of the change.

111. You send an email message to your friend with an invitation to a special event. What do you write?

112. You pass a note in class, to your study partner, reminding her of the details of your next meeting. What do you write?

113. When you do well in your assignments, what does your Spanish teacher write?

114. Your team has won an important match in a competition. What is written on the notice board commending your performance?

115. You want to go and see a particular movie, but don't know which cinema is showing it. What text message do you send to your friend who should have this information?

116. You have done badly on a test. What does your teacher write to encourage you?

117. Your friend comes to pick you up to go out, but tells you that plans have changed. What note do you leave for your parents, indicating where you have gone?

118. You have not been doing your chores at home and your parents insist that you write a note with a commitment. What do you write?

119. Your grandmother arrives unexpectedly from the country and finds no one at home. What note does she leave, saying where she can be reached?

120. You have had a delicious meal in a fine restaurant and want to send a note to the chef along with a tip. What do your write?

121. There is a competition at school for the best teacher of the year. What reason do you write to justify your choice?

122. Your aunt will be visiting from abroad and sends an email message with her arrival information. What does she write?

123. You need your mother to pick you up at a different time from usual. What information do you text her?

124. Your neighbour comes to visit you but no one is at home. What short note does he/she leave on the door about a community event?

125. Your Spanish teacher has to be away. What information does she leave about the work that the class is to do?

126.     You purchase an item for your brother, but it does not fit. What information does he leave with the item, to help you make the exchange?

127.     You are having a headache and you want your mother to buy some medication on her way home. What text message do you send her, expressing your request?

128.     You arrive at a function, only to find the place closed. What notice do you see on the door giving an explanation?

129.     A relative of your best friend has died. What sympathy note do your send your friend?

# LETTERS/COMPOSITIONS
GENERAL PROFICIENCY

This section corresponds to
**Paper 2, Section 2 and is worth 30 marks**

# LETTERS

Write a letter in SPANISH of 130-150 words AND NO MORE. Use the tense or tenses appropriate to the topic.

1.  You want to spend summer in a Spanish-speaking country. Write a letter to a lady you have heard about who offers accommodation and include

    (i)    personal information about yourself
    (ii)   your reasons for wanting to visit
    (iii)  a request for the cost of accommodation
    (iv)   your travel plans.

2.  A friend of yours wants to spend his/her holidays in the Spanish-speaking country you visited last year. Write a letter to your host family and mention

    (i)    information about your friend
    (ii)   why your friend wants to spend summer there
    (iii)  suggestions for activities that would interest your friend
    (iv)   some changes in the living arrangements that would make your friend more comfortable.

3.  You arranged to spend three months with a family in a Spanish-speaking country. You were unhappy there and returned home early. Write a letter to your hosts and include

    (i)    the reasons for your unhappiness
    (ii)   your appreciation of their efforts to make you comfortable
    (iii)  what your trip home was like
    (iv)   how you will spend your time, now that you are home.

4.  You are working part-time in a hotel. Write a reply to a letter from someone in a Spanish-speaking country who has requested information about a holiday in your country. Include

    (i)    some information about the hotel
    (ii)   the attractions that are nearby
    (iii)  some of the tours that are available
    (iv)   an offer to provide additional information.

5.  You are on an exchange programme in a Spanish-speaking country. Write a letter to your sister who is also studying Spanish and mention

    (i)    your lost luggage
    (ii)   the help you received from your host family
    (iii)  what you bought when you went shopping
    (iv)   how much you miss your family and friends.


6.  You are planning to return to the Spanish-speaking country you visited last year. Write a letter to your friend in that country. Include

    (i)    your reasons for returning
    (ii)   details about your arrival
    (iii)  suggestions as to what you want to do this time
    (iv)   greetings to other friends.


7.  Your parents have agreed that you can complete high school in a Spanish-speaking country. Write a letter to your pen pal in Venezuela and mention

    (i)    why you want to study there
    (ii)   your academic achievements
    (iii)  your extra-curricular interests
    (iv)   when you wish to attend.


8.  You have just bought a new pet which you are enjoying very much. Write a letter to your friend in a Spanish-speaking country telling him/her

    (i)    what kind of pet you have bought
    (ii)   what your family thinks of it
    (iii)  how you take care of your pet
    (iv)   your hope that he/she will see it one day.


9.  Your father has just got a new job and your family will be in a Spanish-speaking country for one year. Write a letter to your friend in that country in which you

    (i)    tell him/her the news
    (ii)   explain what your father will be doing there
    (iii)  say what you are looking forward to seeing
    (iv)   express your hope to spend some time with him/her.

10. Your cousin who lives in a Spanish-speaking country has sent a ticket for you to spend the Summer holidays with him/her. Write a letter in which you

    (i)   thank him/her for the kindness
    (ii)  express your happiness
    (iii) tell him/her some of the things you want to do when you get there
    (iv)  express your hope to see him/her soon.


11. You have just had a short story published in the newspaper. Write a letter to your former Spanish teacher who is studying in a Spanish-speaking country and

    (i)   tell him/her the good news
    (ii)  describe what the story is about
    (iii) say whether or not you plan to write more stories in the future
    (iv)  promise to send him/her a copy.


12. Your penpal who lives in a Spanish-speaking country writes to tell you that he/she was placed first in the end of year examinations in school. Write a letter in which you

    (i)   congratulate him/her
    (ii)  ask for more information about the examinations
    (iii) tell him/her how you feel about examinations
    (iv)  wish him/her success in future examinations.

# COMPOSITIONS

Write a composition in SPANISH of 130-150 words AND NO MORE. Use the tense or tenses appropriate to the topic.

I.    You spent your summer holidays in a Spanish-speaking country. Write a composition in which you mention

    (i)    the reasons you chose that country

    (ii)   some of the places you visited

    (iii)  an embarrassing incident in which you were involved

    (iv)   what you liked most about the people.


2.    During your stay in a Spanish-speaking country you plan a surprise birthday party for your room-mate. Write a composition describing

    (i)    the arrangements you made to get your room-mate out of the house

    (ii)   the food and drinks you prepared for the party

    (iii)  the reaction of your room-mate on returning home

    (iv)   the fun you had.


3.    While vacationing in a Spanish-speaking country you rented a car and were involved in an accident. Describe

    (i)    the village you were driving through

    (ii)   what caused the accident

    (iii)  the help you received from other drivers

    (iv)   the drive to the hospital in the ambulance.


4.    You spent a weekend in a Spanish-speaking country. Write a composition and describe

    (i)    your arrival at the airport in that country

    (ii)   a delicious meal you had

    (iii)  some gifts that you bought

    (iv)   what you enjoyed most about the trip.

5.   While visiting a Spanish-speaking country, you and your friends went by train to another city. Write a composition and describe

   (i)    your late arrival at the train station
   (ii)   the group activities on the train
   (iii)  an unexpected stop
   (iv)   how you felt when you reached your destination.


6.   You are studying in a Spanish-speaking country. Your teacher tells you to write a composition about life in your country and to describe

   (i)    your family
   (ii)   a typical dish
   (iii)  some of the popular recreational activities
   (iv)   some places of interest.


7.   You have been chosen to do a presentation about your school to some Spanish-speaking exchange students. Write a composition in which you include

   (i)    the name and size of your school
   (ii)   the history of your school
   (iii)  some of the clubs and extra-curricular activities
   (iv)   what you like most about your school.


8.   While you are on holidays in a Spanish-speaking country, you are asked to speak about your favourite tourist attraction in your country. Write a composition in which you include

   (i)    the name and location of the place
   (ii)   a description of the place
   (iii)  how often you visit it
   (iv)   what you like most about the place.


9.   While you are vacationing in a Spanish-speaking country, you have been asked to speak about a camp you recently attended. Write a composition in which you include

   (i)    the reason you attended the camp
   (ii)   some of the activities which took place during the camp
   (iii)  the most exciting day of the camp
   (iv)   what you liked most about the camp.

10. While you are attending school in a Spanish-speaking country you enter a competition in which you must describe your neighbourhood. Write a composition in which you describe

    (i)    the location of your neighbourhood
    (ii)   whal the public service facilities are like
    (iii)  what the people are like
    (iv)   some outstanding fcatures of the neighbourhood.


11. Your family is living in a Spanish-speaking country for a year and your father has been involved in an accident to which you were a witness. Write a composition about

    (i)    the vehicles which were involved in the accident
    (ii)   the time the accident occurred
    (iii)  what your father was doing when it happened
    (iv)   the results of the accident.


12. You have just returned from a visit to a Spanish-speaking country. Write a composition in which you

    (i)    explain the reason for your trip
    (ii)   describe the persons who accompanied you
    (iii)  tell about a well-known tourist attraction there
    (iv)   relate an incident in the airport when you were returning.

# CONTEXTUAL ANNOUNCEMENTS/CONTEXTUAL DIALOGUES

## GENERAL PROFICIENCY

This section corresponds to
**Paper 2 Section 3 and is worth 20 marks.**

# CONTEXTUAL ANNOUNCEMENTS

Use the following cues to write an announcement of about 80 – 100 words in Spanish.

Your youth club has planned a sale of used books to raise funds for an important cause. Write the announcement which has been placed in different parts of the community.

Be sure to include ALL the cues listed below in the announcement

i]      An invitation to students to come and purchase their books

ii]     The cause which the book sales will benefit

iii]    The four subjects for which books will be available

iv]     Two reasons it is better for students to buy books at that sale

v]      The grades for which books will be available.


## MODEL ANSWER 1

- *El Club Estrella invita a todos los estudiantes a una venta masiva e importante. Vengan a comprar libros usados a buenos precios.*
- *Las ganancias de esta venta serán usadas para comprar comida y ropa para donar a los pobres de nuestra comunidad.*
- *Habrá libros para química, historia, geografía y ciencia.*
- *Los libros usados son más baratos que los libros nuevos en las librerías. Además tenemos una variedad más amplia de libros.*
- *Tenemos libros para estudiantes de primer, segundo, tercer y cuarto grados.*
- *Uds necesitan aprovecharse de esta oportunidad.*


## MODEL ANSWER 2

*El Club Estrella invita a todos los estudiantes a una venta masiva e importante. Vengan a comprar libros usados a buenos precios. Las ganancias de esta venta serán usadas para comprar comida y ropa para donar a los pobres de nuestra comunidad. Habrá libros para química, historia, geografía y ciencia. Los libros usados son más baratos que los libros nuevos en las librerías. Además tenemos una variedad más amplia de libros. Tenemos libros para estudiantes de primer, segundo, tercer y cuarto grados. Uds necesitan aprovecharse de esta oportunidad.*

1. Use the cues provided to complete an announcement of about 80-100 words in Spanish.

   The owner of a store that sells school supplies, has a sale and is encouraging students to take advantage of the low prices. Write the notice that is placed on the Notice Board at your school.

   Be sure to include ALL the cues listed below in the announcement.

   - i]    The name of the store and its location.
   - ii]   Three items that are on sale.
   - iii]  Three advantages of shopping at the store.
   - iv]   How long the sale will last.
   - v]    An invitation to come to the store.

2. Use the cues provided to complete an announcement of about 80-100 words in Spanish.

   You and a group of friends have formed a new club at your school. You need to get more members to join the club and place an announcement on the Notice Board at your school.

   Be sure to include ALL the cues listed below in the announcement.

   - i]    The name of the new club.
   - ii]   When and where you meet.
   - iii]  The purpose of your new club.
   - iv]   Three activities that you will do in this club.
   - v]    An invitation to attend club meetings.

3. Use the cues provided to complete an announcement of about 80-100 words in Spanish.

   The Charity Club at your school is having a special drive to collect items for elderly people in your community. As secretary, write the announcement you place on the notice board encouraging your schoolmates to participate.

   Be sure to include ALL the cues listed below in the announcement.

   - i]    A special name for the project.
   - ii]   The purpose of the project.
   - iii]  Three types of items you will accept for the project.
   - iv]   Where students should deliver their contributions.
   - v]    An encouragement to everyone to participate.

4.  Use the cues provided to complete an announcement of about 80-100 words in Spanish.

Your class is planning a trip to celebrate the end of the term. Your teacher has asked you to place an announcement on the notice board to update the class about the plans.

Be sure to include ALL the cues listed below.

    i]     The date and destination of the trip.
    ii]    The cost.
    iii]   Plans for lunch.
    iv]   Four activities you will do on the trip.
    v]    An encouragement for all your classmates to take part.

5.  Use the cues provided to complete an announcement of about 80-100 words in Spanish.

The Spanish club is having a Spanish film festival to raise money. Write the announcement you place as President of the club on the Notice Board.

Be sure to include ALL the cues listed below in the announcement.

    i]     The date and venue of the film festival.
    ii]    The name of two Spanish films that will be shown.
    iii]   Two reasons you need to raise money.
    iv]   Three reasons everyone will enjoy the film.
    v]    An invitation to everyone to see the film.

6.  Use the cues provided to complete an announcement of about 80-100 words in Spanish.

The Spanish Club at your school is holding elections to choose new leaders. Write the announcement which you, as outgoing secretary, place on the Notice Board.

Be sure to include ALL the cues listed below in the announcement.

    i]     The purpose of the elections.
    ii]    The date, time and venue of the elections.
    iii]   The importance of participating in the elections.
    iv]   The qualities a good leader should have.
    v]    An encouragement for everyone to participate.

7.  Use the cues provided to complete an announcement of about 80-100 words in Spanish.

The students Council is planning a concert to raise funds for some special projects in the school. Write the announcement you placed on the Notice Board.

Be sure to include ALL the cues listed below in the announcement.

    i]     A name for the concert.
    ii]    The date, time and venue.
    iii]   Three projects that will benefit by the concert.
    iv]   Three exciting items that will be on the programme.
    v]    The invitation to attend the concert.

8. Use the cues provided to complete an announcement of about 80-100 words in Spanish.

Your favourite teacher has recently published a book. You want the entire school to know about it so you place an announcement on the Notice Board, encouraging everyone to buy and read this book.

Be sure to include ALL the cues listed below in the announcement.

  i]   The title and author of the book.
  ii]  Where the book can be obtained.
  iii] What the book is about.
  iv]  Three reasons you think the book is good.
  v]   Three adjectives to describe the book.

9. Use the cues provided to complete an announcement of about 80-100 words in Spanish.

You have planned a day of culture to highlight the different foods, drinks and customs of the Caribbean. Write the announcement you put up in different places in the school, encouraging the students to participate.

Be sure to include ALL the cues listed below in the announcement.

  i]   The date, time and venue of the cultural show.
  ii]  The purpose of the cultural show.
  iii] Three ways in which students can participate.
  iv]  Three ways in which students can benefit by the cultural show.
  v]   The reason the show is free of cost.

10. Use the cues provided to complete an announcement of about 80-100 words in Spanish.

As the President of the Speech Club at your school you have invited a very important person in your country to deliver a speech to your Club. However, you want as many persons as possible from your school to listen to the speech. Write an announcement for the main Notice Board.

Be sure to include ALL the cues listed below in the announcement.

  i]   The name of the important person.
  ii]  The date, time and venue of the speech.
  iii] Three reasons students at your school should not miss the speech.
  iv]  Three important facts about the person that will convince students to listen to the speech.
  v]   An invitation for all students to attend.

# CONTEXTUAL DIALOGUES

## Examples 1

1.    You have lost your puppy and you are trying to find it.  Using 80 – 100 words, complete the dialogue you have with one of your neighbours, **giving your replies**.

Responses to all of the cues listed below MUST be included in the completed dialogue.

(i)     Greetings
(ii)    Reason for the problem
(iii)   Who gave you the gift
(iv)    Neighbour's advice
(v)     Agreement and thanks
(vi)    Leave taking


VECINO:    Buenas tardes, joven, ¿Qué te pasa?
YO:        *Buenas tardes, Señor, es que no puedo encontrar mi perrito.  Parece que está perdido.*

VECINO:    Lo siento mucho, pero no recuerdo haber visto un perro extranjero por aquí. ¿Cómo es tu perro?
YO:        *Pués, Señor, mi perrito es negro y blanco.*

VECINO:    ¿Por qué no andas a todas las casas en la vecindad y preguntas por tu perrito?
YO:        *He hablado con todos los vecinos en la calle y nadie ha visto mi perrito.*

VECINO:    ¡Qué raro!  ¿Nadie en la vecindad lo ha visto?  ¿Quién te compró el perrito? ¿Tus padres?
YO:        *No, Señor, es un regalo de mis abuelos.  Me lo regalaron para mi cumpleaños.*

VECINO:    ¡Qué suerte! Claro, tus abuelos te quieren mucho para comprarte un regalo tan especial.  ¿Qué piensas hacer ahora en cuanto al perrito perdido?
YO:        *Pienso poner anuncios por toda la vecindad.*

VECINO:    Buena idea, poner anuncios.  Yo voy a ayudarte preguntando a las personas que conozco si han visto el perrito.
YO:        *Gracias por su ayuda, Señor.*

| VECINO: | Recuerda incluir tu dirección y número de teléfono en los anuncios. |
| YO: | *Lo voy a hacer, Señor.* |

| VECINO: | Eres muy cortés joven. Llámame a fines de esta semana para decirme qué tal la situación, si has encontrado tu perro. |
| YO : | *Le llamo este fin de semana para informle de la situación. Me voy ahora.*   *Que le vaya bien y gracias por su interés, señor.* |

| VECINO: | Suerte con la búsqueda. Espero tu llamada o visita. Yo haré mi parte. |
| YO: | *Adiós, Señor.* |

## Example 2

2.   You and your classmate have a discussion concerning  what you like or dislike about your school. Using 80 – 100 words, complete the dialogue you have with your school-friend, **giving your replies.**

Responses to all the cues listed below MUST be included in the completed dialogue.

   (i)     The subject that is disliked most
   (ii)    The problems with the cafeteria
   (iii)   What the students in the class are like
   (iv)   The Sports programme
   (v)    Dealing with a busy schedule
   (vi)   Leave taking

| COLEGA: | No puedo soportar esta escuela y la clase de matemáticas es terrible. Hay demasiado trabajo.  ¿Qué piensas? |
| YO: | *A decir verdad, me encanta esta asignatura y la profesora es muy simpática.* |

| COLEGA: | ¿Qué estás diciendo?  ¿Que te gusta una asignatura si la profesora es amable? |
| YO: | *Sí, la profesora hace una diferencia.* |

| COLEGA: | Pero no es sólo las asignaturas que me molestan, la comida en la cafetería es cada día peor.  ¿Todavía comes allá? |
| YO: | *Sí, porque el pollo con papas fritas es sabroso.* |

COLEGA: ¿Así que te gusta la escuela porque hay platos en la cafetería que son deliciosos?
YO: *Hay muchos aspectos de la escuela que me gustan.*

COLEGA: ¿Cuáles aspectos de la escuela te gustan?
YO: *Primero, los estudiantes de mi clase son muy simpáticos y también me encanta el programa de deportes.*

COLEGA: Estoy de acuerdo que los estudiantes de nuestra clase son amables, pero no me interesan los deportes. ¿En cuál deporte participas?
YO: *Participo en el atletismo, el voléibol y el tenis y he ganado muchos premios.*

COLEGA: ¿Tres deportes? ¡Es demasiado! ¿Tienes tiempo para estudiar?
YO: *Sí, preparo un horario y esto me ayuda a organizar mi tiempo.*

COLEGA ¿Me puedes ayudar a preparar un horario?
YO: *¡Cómo no! El gusto es mío. ¿Cuándo tendrás tiempo?*

COLEGA: Mañana después de las clases está perfecto.
YO: *Nos vemos mañana entonces. Adiós, hasta luego.*

3. You are a student at a high school and go to the library to get some information for a project. Using 80 – 100 words, complete the dialogue you have with the librarian, **giving your replies.**

Responses to all of the cues listed below MUST be included in the completed dialogue

   (i)   Greetings
   (ii)  Topic of research
   (iii) How to access information in the Library
   (iv)  Cost of using equipment
   (v)   Role of the Librarian
   (vi)  Leave taking

BIBLIOTECARIA: Buenas tardes, ¿necesitas algo en la biblioteca?
YO: _____
_____

BIBLIOTECARIA: ¿Cuál es el tema de la investigación?
YO: _____
_____

BIBLIOTECARIA: Muy interesante. Tenemos muchos libros sobre las plantas medicinales y también, puedes usar la computadora.
YO: _____
_____

BIBLIOTECARIA: Si, ¡cómo no! Puedes usar libros, computadoras, todo lo que necesitas para la investigación.
YO: _____
_____

BIBLIOTECARIA: Puedes empezar con el católogo que está allá cerca de aquellas estantes.
YO: _____
_____

BIBLIOTECARIA: Las computadoras están en el segundo piso.
YO: _____
_____

BIBLIOTECARIA: No cuesta nada, es gratis. Si quieres imprimir algo, hay que pagar el papel.

YO: _____

_____

BIBLIOTECARIA: El gusto es mío. Estamos aquí para servir al público.

YO: _____

_____

BIBLIOTECARIA: Sí, muchas personas visitan la biblioteca porque necesitan información.

YO: _____

_____


4. You are a student at a high school and you have been sent to the Principal because of problems you are having. Using 80 – 100 words, complete the dialogue you have with the Principal, **giving your replies.**

Responses to all of the cues listed below MUST be included in the completed dialogue.

(i) Reason for being sent to the Principal
(ii) Consequences of not improving
(iii) Participating in the Championship
(iv) Nature of the penalty
(v) Who is to blame


DIRECTOR: ¿Sabes por qué estás aquí en mi oficina?

YO: _____

_____

DIRECTOR: Tu profesora de inglés me dijo que no haces las tareas de casa. ¿Qué te pasa?

YO: _____

_____

DIRECTOR: Si no se mejoran la notas, voy a prohibir que participes en el programa de deportes

YO: _____

_____

DIRECTOR: No importa que hayas ganado tantos trofeos para la escuela, el aspecto académico es muy importante.

YO: _____

_____

DIRECTOR: Está bien, vamos a ver. Tienes sólo tres semanas para mejorar.
YO: _____

_____

DIRECTOR: No, no puedes participar en el campeonato mañana.
YO: _____

_____

DIRECTOR: Si la escuela no gana porque tú no participas, tenemos que aceptar la situación.
YO: _____

_____

DIRECTOR: O.K. Hablaré con tus padres sobre el asunto y después tomaré la decisión .
YO: _____

_____

DIRECTOR: Recuerda que la culpa es tuya y que la decisión es para tu bien.
YO: _____

_____

5. Elena and her mother talk about plans for Elena's birthday party.  Using 80 – 100 words, complete the dialogue Elena has with her mother, **giving Elena's replies**.

Responses to all of the cues listed below MUST be included in the completed dialogue.

(i)     Date of the birthday
(ii)    How the birthday could be celebrated
(iii)   Who should be invited
(iv)    Dinner menu
(v)     Drinks that will be served
(vi)    Appreciation for the gesture

LA MAMA: Elena, ¿recuerdas que tu cumpleaños es el 21 del próximo mes?
ELENA: _____

_____

LA MAMA: Tu papá y yo pensábamos que puedes tener una fiesta.  ¿Qué opinas?
ELENA: _____

_____

LA MAMA: Puedes invitar a los alumnos de tu clase, a unos miembros de la familia, y claro, a unos vecinos …

ELENA: _____

_____

LA MAMA: Unos treinta invitados, pensaba.

ELENA: _____

_____

LA MAMA: Es que no recordaba que había tantos estudiantes en tu clase.

ELENA: _____

_____

LA MAMA: O.K. Podemos invitar a cincuenta personas, total, incluso los miembros de la familia. Está bien.

ELENA: _____

_____

LA MAMA: ¿Qué quieres que preparemos para la cena de cumpleaños?

ELENA: _____

_____

LA MAMA: ¡Perfecto! Y también servimos arroz con frijoles y ensalada.

ELENA: _____

_____

LA MAMA: Ponche de frutas, cervezas y ron para los adultos.

ELENA: _____

_____

6.   Two classmates have to work on a school project together. Using 80 – 100 words, complete the dialogue they have, **giving Roberto's replies.**

Responses to all of the cues listed below MUST be included in the completed dialogue.

   (i)      Division of responsibilities
   (ii)     Where to access information
   (iii)    When it is convenient to meet
   (iv)    Final decisions about meeting
   (v)     Where they will meet
   (vi)    What food will be provided

LIANA: Hola, Roberto, según la profesora, los dos tenemos que trabajar juntos en el proyecto de ciencia.

ROBERTA: _____

_____

LIANA: Pues, primero, hay que decidir qué parte cada persona va a hacer.

ROBERTO: _____

_____

LIANA: O.K. Está bien. Si tu prefieres buscar información en el Internet, yo iré a la biblioteca y usaré los libros allá.

ROBERTO: _____

_____

LIANA: Sólo tengo tiempo libre los fines de semana, porque tengo actividades co-curriculares lunes a viernes.

ROBERTO: _____

_____

LIANA: Así que ¿nos quedamos en reunirnos los sábados de este mes, desde las dos hasta las seis de la tarde?

ROBERTO: _____

_____

LIANA: ¿Te conviene venir a mi casa? Vivo cerca de la escuela.

ROBERTO: _____

_____

LIANA: Perfecto, así puedes caminar a mi casa.

ROBERTO: _____

_____

LIANA: Mi mamá va a prepararnos una comida. ¿Qué te gustaría comer?

ROBERTO: _____

_____

LIANA: Me encanta este mismo plato también. ¡Qué chévere!

ROBERTO: _____

_____

7. Two friends have a telephone conversation to make arrangements to go out together and to study. Using 80 – 100 words, complete the dialogue they have, **giving Sergio's responses.**

Responses to all of the cues listed below MUST be included in the completed dialogue.

    (i)        Greetings on the phone
    (ii)       Invitation refused
    (iii)     Agreement to study
    (iv)     Arrangements to pick up Sergio
    (v)      Persons who will go out on Saturday
    (vi)    Confirmation of arrangements and leave taking

LINDA:    Bueno, casa de los Monteros.
SERGIO:   _____
                 _____

LINDA:    Hola Sergio, ¿qué tal estás?
SERGIO:   _____
                 _____

LINDA:    Gracias por la invitación Sergio, pero es que había pensado estudiar este sábado. Tengo que hacer un proyecto.
SERGIO:   _____
                 _____

LINDA:    Pues, sí, pudiera cambiar de idea y estudiar otro día. ¿Quieres estudiar conmigo?
SERGIO:   _____
                 _____

LINDA:    El domingo después de la iglesia es conveniente. ¿Qué tal a las diez?
SERGIO:   _____
                 _____

LINDA:    Mi papá puede pasar por ti a las diez de la mañana. ¿Está bien?
SERGIO:   _____
                 _____

LINDA:    Así que ¿otros amigos nos van a acompañar el sábado?
SERGIO:   _____
                 _____

LINDA: No los he visto hace más de dos semanas. Tengo muchas ganas de verlos.

SERGIO: _____

_____

LINDA: Pues, me encanta el plan, Sergio. Nos vemos pronto y gracias por la llamada.

SERGIO: _____

_____

8. Two friends chat on-line about an incident which was reported in the newspaper, which one of them witnessed. Using 80 – 100 words, complete the dialogue they have, **giving Vérica's replies.**

Responses to all of the cues listed below MUST be included in the completed dialogue.

(i) What was reported
(ii) What really happened
(iii) The role of the police
(iv) What Vérica did
(v) Reaction to Vérica's actions
(vi) Leave taking

PATRICIA: ¿Viste el artículo en el diario sobre el robo?

VÉRICA: _____

_____

PATRICIA: Sí, ese mismo. ¿Sabes lo que realmente ocurrió?

VÉRICA: _____

_____

PATRICIA: Pero, ¿dónde ocurrió el incidente?

VÉRICA: _____

_____

PATRICIA: ¿Y la policía no llegó?

VÉRICA: _____

_____

PATRICIA: ¿Tan tarde? ¿Por qué?

VÉRICA: _____

_____

PATRICIA: Muy interesante, Vérica. Y ¿qué hacías tú?

VÉRICA: _____

_____


PATRICIA: De verdad, eres muy inteligente. ¿Has tenido experiencia en este tipo de situaciones?

VÉRICA: _____

_____


PATRICIA: Pues, no soy valiente y no me gustan las aventuras.

VÉRICA: _____

_____


PATRICIA: Hasta luego Vérica y cuídate mucho.

VÉRICA: _____

_____


9. Two students discuss a class party. Using 80 – 100 words, complete the dialogue they have, **giving Melena's replies.**

Responses to all of the cues listed below MUST be included in the completed dialogue.

(i)     Concern about the plans for the party
(ii)    Offer to help
(iii)   Decisions about food
(iv)    Drinks that can be served
(v)     Arrangements for music
(vi)    Leave taking

ELISA: ¿Cómo van los planes para la fiesta?

MELENA: _____

_____


ELISA: Pero: ¿por qué tu solita estás haciendo todo cuando hay unos cuarenta estudiantes en la clase?

MELENA: _____

_____


ELISA: No te preocupes, amiga, yo voy a ayudarte. Primero hablemos de la comida. ¿Qué vamos a servir?

MELENA: _____

_____

ELISA: ¡Estupendo! A todo el mundo le gusta este plato. ¿Y para beber?

MELENA: _____

_____

ELISA: ¿Se permite servir esta clase de bebidas en la escuela?

MELENA: _____

_____

ELISA: Mejor hablemos de esto con la profesora. ¿Tienes música?

MELENA: _____

_____

ELISA: Parece bien y mi hermano tiene música de salsa y de merengue que voy a traer.

MELENA: _____

_____

ELISA: Pues amiga, ¡ Imagínate! ¡Hemos planeado la fiesta en unos pocos minutos!

MELENA: _____

_____

ELISA: Me voy ahora, amiga, nos vemos pronto

MELENA: _____

_____

# READING COMPREHENSION
## GENERAL PROFICIENCY

Candidates are required to answer questions based on a continuous passage.

Questions will be in English and answers are to be written in English. This section corresponds to **Paper 2, Section 4 and is worth 20 marks**.

**Read the passage carefully and then answer the questions in English.**

- ¡Eres muy malo! ¡Eres muy necio! gritó el papá de Pepito. Pepito había roto un florero de cristal que pertenecía a la abuela de su papá. Su papá estaba muy enojado porque Pepito siempre rompía algún objeto de gran valor en la casa.

Pepito decidió que iba a huir de casa. No le gustaba que su padre le gritara. Se sentía muy mal porque había roto algo con tanto valor.

Durante la noche cuando todos estaban dormidos, Pepito se levantó y buscó la maleta. Arregló toda la ropa favorita que quería llevar con él. Atravesaba el suelo de puntillas cuando oyó una voz que le decía:
- Si sales de la casa no puedes volver.

Pepito se detuvo. Cuando dio una vuelta completa no vio a nadie pero sabía que era la voz de su papá.

- Te queremos mucho, pero a veces nos ponemos furiosos por tu comportamiento. Es verdad que te gritamos cuando estamos enojados pero esto no quiere decir que no te queramos. Debes tratar de tener más cuidado.

Pepito se quedó pensando. En realidad él no quería huir de la casa. A él le gustaba su casa. Entonces, decidió y les dijo:
- No, no voy a salir. Voy a quedarme aquí, voy a tratar de tener cuidado y de ser más agradable.

## Questions

1. Why did Pepito's father shout at him?
2. To whom did the vase belong?
3. What was Pepito planning to do?
4. When did Pepito get up and why?
5. What did he decide to put in the suitcase?
6. Who spoke to him when he was about to leave?
7. What did Pepito like?
8. What was Pepito's decision?
9. Why did he take that decision?
10. State your opinion of the decision.

**Read the passage carefully and then answer the questions in English.**

Ayer, por la mañana, dos hombres vestidos de gris, entraron en una joyería situada en el centro de la ciudad, cerca de la Avenida Tijuana.

Según un testigo que estaba en la joyería durante el atraco, uno de los hombres se acercó al gerente de la joyería y le ordenó que le diera todas las joyas que estaban en la vitrina. Además, los clientes tenían que quitarse sus propias joyas y ponerlas en un saco que el otro ladrón llevaba. Lo raro era que el guardia que trabajaba para la empresa, sacó un revólver y disparó dos veces. Una de las balas hirió al gerente en la rodilla.

Los tres salieron con una cantidad de joyas incluso relojes suizos de primera calidad, pendientes y anillos de oro. Escaparon en un auto que les esperaba afuera con el motor arrancado. La policía sigue buscando a los ladrones y pide al público que le dé cualquier información que tenga. También hay una recompensa para quien tenga información acerca del asunto.

**Questions**

1. When did the robbery occur?
2. Where is the jewellery store located?
3. What did the robber order the manager to do?
4. What did the clients have to do?
5. Why did the action of the person with the revolver seem strange?
6. What happened to the manager of the jewellery store?
7. What types of jewellery did the robbers take?
8. How did the robbers make their escape?
9. What is the police requesting?
10. What do you think of the robbers' plan? Give your reason(s)

**Read the passage carefully and then answer the questions in English.**

*Querida Lourdes,*

*Aquí estamos en México y lo estamos pasando bien. El domingo fuimos a Izamal en tren y fue un viaje maravilloso.*

*Llegamos a la estación de Mérida a las siete de la mañana y el tren arrancó media hora después de nuestra llegada.*

*El viaje duró dos horas y al llegar a nuestro destino, había una banda de músicos para entretenernos. Además, el director de turismo de Izamal estaba en la estación para darnos la bienvenida.*

*Recorrimos todo el pueblo en calesas que son bonitos carros de muchos colores tirados por caballos. Vimos la iglesia más vieja de la Provincia, unos edificios antiguos y la artesanía de los indios. Te compré un regalo. Almorzamos a la una y la comida estaba muy sabrosa. Yo comí pollo con salsa verde y de postre, helado de vainilla y pastel.*

*Así que, Lourdes, este intercambio de estudiantes me ha ayudado muchísimo. Ojalá tú estés aprendiendo mucho inglés en Jamaica y divirtiéndote tanto como yo.*

*Escríbeme pronto y saluda a todos de mi parte.*

*Recibe un abrazo cariñoso de tú amiga,*
*Kelly-Ann*

**Questions**

1. How did the visitors get to Izamal?
2. At what time did the journey start?
3. When did they arrive at Izamal?
4. Who were the persons in the station to greet the travelers?
5. Describe the 'calesas'.
6. What did they see on the tour of the city?
7. After eating chicken, what else did Kelly-Ann eat?
8. How was the lunch?
9. What is Lourdes doing in Jamaica?
10. What do you think of Lourdes' activities? Explain your reply.

**Read the passage carefully and then answer the questions in English.**

Una tarde después de un almuerzo grande de mosquitos y moscas Moho, el sapo, se escondió al lado de la charca para dormir la siesta. Estaba soñando con la cena cuando de repente se despertó asustado. Sentía algo en la espalda. ¿Será una hoja? se preguntó. De pronto oyó un sonido que reconoció como la voz del niño que siempre jugaba en la charca. Muy lentamente abrió los ojos y vio la cara de un ser humano. ¡Qué horror! Se dio cuenta de que el niño lo había atrapado.

Moho se dijo - ¡Qué niño atrevido! Me despertó de la siesta para que jugara con él. Es obvio que está cansado de los peces y quiere molestarme. Se acordó de la última vez que una niña lo había capturado. Ella lo llevó a su casa donde pasó dos días. Fueron los peores días de su vida. La niña no le permitió buscar las moscas para la comida y casi se murió de hambre. Cuando logró escaparsé juró que nunca volvería a la casa de otro ser humano y ahora le iba a pasar el mismo horror....

## Questions

1. Why did the toad go into hiding?
2. What was the toad doing before he was awakened?
3. How did he wake up?
4. Why did he think there was a leaf on his back?
5. Who was making noises/sounds?
6. What did this person like to do?
7. Who had caught the toad before?
8. When did the toad spend the worst of his life?
9. If you were the toad, what would you do now?
10. What can the toad really do?

**Read the passage carefully and then answer the questions in English.**

El Hermano Anansi y el Herrnano Pájaro eran grandes enemigos. El Hermano Pájaro siempre se quejaba del día cuando el Hermano Anansi le engañó y le dijo a todo el mundo que El Hermano Anansi nunca tendría la oportunidad de volver a hacerlo.

El Hermano Anansi dijo que estaba harto de las quejas del Hermano Pájaro y decidió que iba a mostrarle que era el Rey de las trampas y que podía burlarse de una persona muchas veces.

Mandó a decirle al Hermano Pájaro que su mamá había muerto y que necesitaba su ayuda con el funeral. El Hermano Pájaro era muy simpático y se decidió a ayudar a Anansi.

Mientras esperaba la llegada del Hermano Pájaro. Anansi se vistió de la ropa de su mamá y se tumbó en la cama.

Cuando el Hermano Pájaro llegó a la casa del Hermano Anansi una de sus hermanas le recibió y le mostró a la mamá en la cama.
　　　– Lo siento mucho – le dijo el Hermano Pájaro
En ese momento el Hermano Anansi se levantó y le dijo tranquilamente:
　　　– Deja de decirle a todo el mundo que yo soy malo.
El Hermano Pájaro se asustó y gritó con temor. Cuando se dio cuenta de que el Hermano Anansi le había engañado otra vez, juró que nunca volvería a hablar ni con él, ni con los otros miembros de su familia.

**Questions**

1.　What was the relationship between Hermano Anansi and Hermano Pájaro like?
2.　What did Hermano Pájaro believe that Hermano Anansi could not do to him again?
3.　What did Hermano Anansi decide to do?
4.　What was Hermano Pájaro like?
5.　How did Hermano Pájaro react when he thought that Hermano Anansi's mother was dead?
6.　Who was in bed?
7.　Why was Hermano Pájaro frightened?
8.　What did Hermano Pájaro decide to do?
9.　In your opinion, was this a good decision?
10.　What advice would you give to Hermano Pájaro, and why?

**Read the passage carefully and then answer the questions in English.**

La familia de Carmen vivía en un pueblo pequeño y bello. Allí había todas las comodidades de la vida moderna. A los padres les encantaba su casa. La compraron de una anciana cuyos bisabuelos la construyeron durante el siglo 19. Los visitantes del pueblo siempre se detenían enfrente de la casa para sacar fotos y siempre comentaban la belleza de la casa. Pero Carmen y su familia tenían un problema serio – los vecinos ruidosos.

Los vecinos se levantaban cada día gritando y peleando. Además armaban mucho bullicio mientras se peleaban entre ellos. La familia de Carmen pensaba mudarse pero no querían dejar su casa preciosa.

Un día, se le ocurrió una idea al papá y la compartió con la familia. Iba a pasar una semana grabando todo el ruido que venía de la casa de los vecinos. Después tocaría la grabación para que los vecinos la escucharan.

Cuando los vecinos escucharon la grabación, se sintieron muy avergonzados y desde ese día cesaron de hacer tanto ruido. La vecindad volvió a estar tranquila y la familia de Carmen decidió quedarse en su casa encantadora.

**Questions**

1. What was the town like?
2. What did Carmen's parents like to do?
3. Who constructed the house in which the family used to live?
4. What did the tourist do?
5. Why was the family planning to move house?
6. What did the father decide to do?
7. What was the effect of the recording on the neighbours?
8. Why did Carmen's family decide to stay?
9. Do you agree with the family's decision? Explain your answer.
10. What would you do if you were in the family's position?

**Read the passage carefully and then answer the questions in English.**

Un día el Hermano Tacumá decidió cultivar un huerto delante de su casa. Decidió hacerlo porque a veces la situación del país se ponía muy dura y la gente padecía de hambre. El Hermano Tacumá quería tener una gran abundancia de comida para venderla y para dársela a los pobres.

El huerto era muy hermoso. Había mucho maíz, frijoles y zanahorias. El Hermano Anansi visitaba al Hermano Tacumá con mucha frecuencia y siempre admiraba el huerto. Él no quería sembrar su propio huerto proque a él no le gustaba trabajar. Nunca había trabajado en la vida. Él deseaba comer las verduras que había en el huerto del Hermano Tacumá. Sin embargo, sabía que el Hermano Tacumá no les daría la comida a las personas perezosas como él. Entonces decidió volver al huerto durante la noche para recoger los productos del huerto del Hermano Tacumá.

Un día, el Hermano Tacumá se dio cuenta de que alguien le robaba las verduras por la noche. Decidió consultar al Hermano Anansi, quien era famoso en toda la región por su inteligencia.

El Hermano Anansi expresó sorpresa cuando escuchó el problema del Hermano Tacumá. Dijo que los ladrones eran sus peores enemigos. El Hermano Tacumá estaba contento cuando escuchó el consejo del Hermano Anansi. Pensó que fue una buena idea contratar a un guardia para cuidar el huerto durante la noche – como le recomendó el Hermano Anansi. Estaba muy contento cuando el Hermano Anansi se ofreció para hacer el trabajo.

## Questions

1. Where did Hermano Tacumá have his vegetable garden?
2. What did he plan to do with the vegetables?
3. What did Hermano Anansi do when he visited Hermano Tacumá?
4. What did Hermano Anansi not want to do?
5. What did Hermano Tacumá discover?
6. Why did Hermano Tacumá consult with Hermano Anansi?
7. What advice did Hermano Anansi give to Hermano Tacumá?
8. Why was Hermano Tacumá happy?
9. What is your impression of Hermano Tacumá?
10. Why do you think Hermano Anansi offered to do the job?

**Read the passage carefully and then answer the questions in English.**

El verano pasado Raúl pasó las vacaciones con los abuelos en el campo. Todos los días se levantaba muy temprano para pasearse por la finca grande de los abuelos. Pasaba todas las mañanas mirando los pájaros, trepando los árboles y jugando con los barcos de papel en la pequeña charca que estaba en la granja. Se divertía de esta manera hasta que la abuela lo llamaba para desayunar.

Le gustaba mucho la comida que la abuela preparaba. Siempre le decía a ella que era la mejor cocinera del mundo. Toda la comida era deliciosa especialmente el pollo frito.

Todos los días después del desayuno, Raul saliá con el abuelo, para atender los animales. Primero, el abuelo les daba de comer a los cerdos. Había más de veinte cerdos gordos y a Raúl le fascinaba ver las colitas que tenían forma de "s". Después iban a dar el maíz a las gallinas.

Un día el abuelo le dijo a Raúl que no se sentía bien y que quería que Raúl fuera a atender Ias gallinas. Raúl estaba contento porque quería demostrar al abuelo que era responsable. Salió corriendo de la casa.

Estaba a punto de abrir la puerta del gallinero cuando vio algo en el rincón. Se asustó cuando se dio cuenta de que era una culebra. No sabía qué hacer. No quería correr porque no quería atraer la culebra con los ruidos:

¿Qué voy a hacer? se preguntó. Se quedó ahí esperando y mirando los ojos espantosos de la culebra.

Después de un rato, oyó una risa que venía de afuera. Fue la voz de José, uno de los labradores quien le preguntó:
- ¿Qué pasa Raúl, tienes miedo de la goma?

## Questions

1. What did Raúl do last Summer?
2. What did he usually do everyday?
3. How did he spend his mornings?
4. What was his opinion of his grandmother?
5. What did his uncle want Raúl to do one day?
6. How did Raúl react and why?
7. What did Raúl see in the chicken house?
8. What did he do while he waited?
9. Why did José laugh at Raúl?
10. How would you describe José's reaction?

**Read the passage carefully and then answer the questions in English.**

Hacía tres semanas que el Hermano Anansi trabajaba en el huerto del Hermano Tacumá como guardia. Todos los días le decía al Hermano Tacumá que le gustaba su trabajo y que él era un buen jefe.

Pero había un problema – los robos continuaban. Un día el Hermano Anansi le dijo al Hermano Tacumá que él había visto al ladrón durante la noche pero no pudo detenerlo.

El Hermano Tacumá fue a consultar al Hermano Pájaro quien le dijo que en su opinión el Hermano Anansi era un gran bandido y que necesitaba emplear a un guardia para vigilar al Hermano Anansi. Él se ofreció para ayudar al Hermano Tacumá a montar una trampa para los ladrones.

En la noche el Hermano Pájaro fue al huerto y se escondió en un árbol. Cuando el Hermano Anansi llegó no vio al Hermano Pájaro. Anansi empezó a llenar un saco grande de maíz y el Hermano Pájaro voló a llamar al Hermano Tacumá. Cuando regresaron Anansi estaba listo para levantar el saco pesado cuando le gritaron:

- ¡No te muevas ladrón!

## Questions

1. How long did Hermano Anansi work on the farm?
2. What did he always tell Hermano Tacumá?
3. According to Hermano Anansi, what did he witness one night?
4. Who did Hermano Tacumá consult and what was this individual's response?
5. What suggestion did Hermano Pájaro make to Hermano Tacumá?
6. What did they agree to do?
7. Who did something in the night, and what did he do?
8. This individual made a big discovery, what was it?
9. What did the individual do?
10. In your opinion, did Hermano Pájaro and Hermano Tacumá respond wisely to Hermano Anansi? Explain your answer.

**Read the passage carefully and then answer the questions in English.**

A Marcos le encantaban los zapatos. Siempre quería que sus padres le compraran zapatos nuevos. El tenía varios tipos de zapatos – los zapatos para la iglesia y otras ocasiones formales, los zapatos que llevaba para la escuela, y los que llevaba en casa.

A veces cuando los zapatos todavía estaban nuevos él les decía a sus padres que necesitaba zapatos nuevos. Cada vez que le compraban un par nuevo él escondía un par viejo aunque le sirviera todavía.

Un día su mamá descubrió una caja grande en la cual Marcos había escondido todos los zapatos que no quería llevar. Había seis pares de zapatos en buenas condiciones. Se sorprendió mucho de que su hijo vanidoso hubiera escondido los zapatos para obtener zapatos nuevos. Decidió que iba a "hacerle un truco".

Llevó todos los zapatos al zapatero y le dijo que quería que limpiara los zapatos para que parecieran nuevos. Después llevó los zapatos a la casa y le dijo a Marcos que le había comprado unos zapatos nuevos. Marcos inmediatamente se alegró, cambió los zapatos que llevaba y se puso un par de "los nuevos".

Después de un día todos los zapatos que tenía antes desaparecieron. La mamá sonrió y se dijo:
- Un día esos zapatos van a ser nuevos otra vez.

**Questions**

1. What did Marcos like?
2. Why did he have different shoes?
3. What did he do when he received a pair of new shoes?
4. What were the shoes Marcos hid like?
5. What did the mother do with the shoes she found?
6. When Marcus received the shoes he thought were new, what did he do?
7. What did he do with the shoes he had before?
8. What did his mother say to herself?
9. What did she mean?
10. If you were Marcos' mother what would you do?

**Read the passage carefully and then answer the questions in English.**

Llegaron bastante temprano a la playa, como a los ocho de la mañana. Todavía no había nadie allí y el cielo estaba nublado.

Vamos a nadar ahora – dijo Ricardo a sus compañeros.

No quiero – respondió Marianela. El agua va a estar fría. Prefiero esperar hasta las diez.

Bueno, yo te acompaño – dijo Kamal.

Al ver a sus dos amigos entrar en el agua, Marianela cambió de idea y como ya tenía puesto el traje de baño, saltó al agua.

Bajo la superficie del mar veían un mundo maravilloso con peces de colores, unos con colas largas, otros pequeños. De repente apareció un tiburón. Los niños no sabían qué hacer. No podían apartar sus ojos de los dientes agudos. Se dieron cuenta de que habían nadado muy lejos de la playa.

Parecía que el tiburón quería algo y que no era agresivo. Kamal, el más valiente, se acercó al tiburón y lo tocó. Al animal le gustaba la atención y empezó a moverse suavemente. Luego, nadando lentamente, dejó a los niños. Afortunadamente, una canoa con pescadores pasaba cerca de los chicos y los hombres ofrecieron llevarlos a la playa. Los chicos dieron las gracias a los pescadores y decidieron que nunca iban a mencionar a nadie su aventura con el tiburón simpático.

## Questions

1.   What was the weather like when the children arrived at the beach?
2.   Why didn't Marianela want to go into the water?
3.   What made her change her mind?
4.   Describe the fish the children saw in the sea.
5.   What did the children realize when the shark appeared?
6.   How do we know that Kamal is brave?
7.   Who helped the children?
8.   How did the children get back to the beach?
9.   What did the children think of the shark?
10.  What did the children decide?

**Read the passage carefully and then answer the questions in English.**

Yolanda llegó a casa, subió corriendo las escaleras y llamó a la puerta del dormitorio de su hermano. Entró sin esperar respuesta. Su hermano estaba tendido en la cama leyendo y escuchando música.

- Por favor, Esteban, quiero que me escuches. Tengo algo muy importante que decirte. Esteban no quería apagar la grabadora pero se dio cuenta de que su hermana menor estaba muy nerviosa y decidió hacerle caso.

- ¿Qué te pasa, Yolanda?
- Pues, esta tarde, camino de la casa, vi algo muy raro en el parque. Había un hombre, vestido de negro, agachado cerca de unas matas. Parecía que trataba de esconder algo, quizás un paquete. Me metí detrás de un árbol y lo miré por unos minutos. Por fin se levantó y salió sin el paquete. Esteban, yo tengo que saber qué hay en el paquete. Los hermanos decidieron salir de la casa durante la noche, cuando sus padres dormían.

Al llegar la hora, los dos salieron de la casa de puntillas y corrieron hacia el parque. Empezaron a buscar el paquete en la oscuridad y acababan de hallarlo cuando, de repente, oyeron unos pasos acercándose rápidamente.

Los jóvenes se asustaron y no sabían qué hacer. Se miraron temblando sin poder hablar. ¡Eran sus padres! Los hermanos tuvieron que regresar a casa inmediatamente, dejando atrás el paquete. Nunca supieron qué había adentro pero todavía creen que era bastante dinero para hacerles ricos durante toda la vida.


## Questions

1.  What did Yolanda do when she climbed the stairs?
2.  What was her brother doing?
3.  Why did Yolanda's brother decide to listen to her?
4.  Why was Yolanda concerned?
5.  What was the man, whom Yolanda saw, doing?
6.  What decision did the children take?
7.  What happened when they found the package?
8.  How did the two children feel?
9.  What happened when their parents arrived?
10. What do the children believe was in the package?

**Read the passage carefully and then answer the questions in English.**

*Mi queridísima tía,*

*No quiero que mi mamá sepa lo que te voy a decir porque va a enojarse, pero ando en apuros.*

*Hace quince días, iba en mi motocicleta cuando de repente apareció un hombre frente a mí. No pude evitarlo. El dijo que estaba en el paso de peatones cuando ocurrió el accidente pero no lo creo. Lo llevaron a la clínica y tengo que pagar las cuentas porque dicen que tengo la culpa.*

*La policía llegó al lugar del accidente y me arrestaron acusándome de ser responsable porque según ellos yo había excedido la velocidad permitida. Estoy seguro que eso tampoco es verdad.*

*Tuve que pasar la noche en la cárcel y me llevaron la mañana siguiente al tribunal. Para colmo de desgracias la juez me acusó de conducir de una manera peligrosa y a una velocidad excesiva y me multó con dos mil quinientos dólares.*

*Por favor tía, ayúdame. También tengo que reparar mi motocicleta, comprar comida y con las otras cuentas necesito diez mil dólares. Te los voy a devolver en cuanto encuentre trabajo. ¡Ojalá sea pronto!*

*Gracias querida tía y espero una carta con el dinero lo antes posible.*

*Recibe un abrazo cariñoso de tu sobrino,*

*Ronaldo*

**Questions**

1. Why does Ronaldo not want his mother to know what happened?
2. Where did the man say he was when the accident occurred?
3. Why does Ronaldo have to pay the bills for the Clinic?
4. How much time did Ronaldo spend locked up?
5. What did the judge say Ronaldo was guilty of?
6. How much did Ronaldo have to pay to the Court?
7. Why does Ronaldo not have money to pay his bills?
8. When is he planning to repay his aunt?
9. When does Ronaldo want to receive the money from his aunt?
10. What do you think of Ronaldo's behaviour? Give your reasons.

**Read the passage carefully and then answer the questions in English.**

El hermano Tigre estaba muy orgulloso de su finca. Las plantas crecían muy rápidamente y él esperaba el día cuando pudiera comer algo que él mismo había cultivado.

Por fin llegó el día cuando decidió que todo estaba listo para recoger la cosecha. Iba a cortar el plátano cuando el plátano le habló tranquilamente diciéndole:

- Haga el favor de no cortarme.

El Hermano Tigre estaba tan asustado que tiró el machete al suelo. Pero, poco después agarró el machete de nuevo para destruir la planta. Al levantar la mano, el machete le habló también y le dijo:

Por favor no me uses para cortarla.

Eso fue demasiado para el Hermano Tigre quien echó a correr. Corrió a toda velocidad hasta la casa del Herrnano Anansi para contarle su fantástica historia. El Hermano Anansi le dio agua fría para calmarle. Después de dos o tres minutos, El Hermano Tigre le contó lo que le había pasado. El Hermano Anansi empezó a reírse. Entonces El Hermano Anansi le dijo al Hermano Tigre que era un cobarde y que era muy estúpido tener miedo de una planta.

Entonces el Hermano Anansi decidió preparar una comida para los dos. Mientras arreglaba la leña para encender el fuego se burlaba del Herrnano Tigre. En medio de las risas, la leña le preguntó:
¿Por qué te burlas del pobre Hermano Tigre?
Dicen que el Hermano Anansi todavía está corriendo.

## Questions

1. What was Hermano Tigre hoping to do?
2. What happened when he was about to harvest the banana?
3. How did Hermano Tigre react?
4. What did he decide after?
5. When he was about to do this, what did the machete do?
6. To whom did he tell the story?
7. What did that person tell him?
8. What reputation does Hermano Anansi have?
9. Explain Hermano Anansi's action.
10. What is your opinion of Hermano Anansi?

**Read the passage carefully and then answer the questions in English.**

Los garífunas constituyen un grupo étnico disperso a lo largo de las costas de cinco países de Centroamérica. No están seguros de todos los detalles precisos de su génesis pero están de acuerdo en que su historia comienza a principios del siglo xvii, cuando dos barcos que transportaban esclavos de África Occidental al Nuevo Mundo naufragaron cerca de San Vicente, en las islas de Barlovento. Los africanos que sobrevivieron fueron acogidos por los indios caribes que habitaban la isla. Con el tiempo ambos grupos se mezclaron y originaron a los garífunas.

Los garífunas a quienes los ingleses llamaban "caribes negros" para distinguirlos de los nativos de América Central, constituyeron un orgulloso pueblo que resistió la colonización por más de cien años. Después de una serie de guerras y levantamientos contra los ingleses, sus principales dirigentes fueron capturados. Los victoriosos ingleses decidieron deportarlos a la inhóspita isla de Roatán, frente a Honduras. Desde allí, los refugiados garífunas se extendieron a distintos lugares de Centroamérica, estableciéndose principalmente en Honduras, Guatemala y Belice, que se denominaba Honduras Británica hasta su independencia en 1981.

En la actualidad alrededor de doscientos mil garífunas viven en Honduras, unos quince mil en Belice, seis mil en Guatemala y otros pocos miles en las Islas de Barlovento y Nicaragua. Aunque estan separados por fronteras nacionales, los garífunas se mantienen unidos en su determinación por preservar su cultura, rica en influencias africanas y americanas.

Las comunidades garífunas conservan celosamente su arte, su música, sus artesanías y sus creencias religiosas, que en conjunto constituyen una forma de vida muy particular.

**Questions**

1. Where are the garífunas to be found?
2. When does the history of the garífunas begin?
3. How did they arrive in St. Vincent?
4. Why did the English call them "Black Caribs"?
5. How did the garífunas arrive in Roatán?
6. How many garífunas live in Guatemala and Belize respectively?
7. What do the garífunas do in their community?
8. Which country has the largest garífuna population?
9. Why do you think they lead private lives?
10. What is the most interesting thing you learnt about the garífunas?

# READING COMPREHENSION
ADDITIONAL EXERCISES

Candidates are required to answer questions based on a variety of written material or graphic stimulus, for example, a continuous passage or an advertisement.

Questions will be in English and answers are to be written in English.

Read the following carefully. DO NOT translate but answer the questions in ENGLISH.

---

### PERSONAL DOMÉSTICO
### EMBAJADA

Necesitamos una persona que tenga experiencia en trabajos domésticos, debe saber atender una mesa y reglas de etiqueta. Buen sueldo, dormir dentro, posibilidad de viajar. Si tienes experiencia comprobable pedir cita por el teléfono 261 0633, horas de oficina.

---

1. What does the applicant need to know?
2. What type of job is this?
3. What is said about accommodation?
4. What kind of experience should the applicant have?
5. How does an interested person apply?

Read the following carefully. DO NOT translate but answer the questions in ENGLISH.

MANTENIMIENTO

IMPERMEABLES
PATO

- LAVAR EN AGUA FRÍA CON JABÓN NEUTRO, AYUDANDO CON UNA ESPONJA.

- NO PLANCHAR.

- NO USAR NUNCA ACETONA NI ALCOHOL.

- DEBE EVITARSE EL CONTACTO CON OBJETOS CALIENTES.

1. What item of clothing is this label from?
2. What should be used to help with washing?
3. What should not be done after washing?
4. What objects should be avoided.
5. Why is alcohol mentioned?

Read the following carefully. DO NOT translate but answer the questions in ENGLISH.

¡CALMA LA PICAZÓN!

Y LA PIEL IRRITADA POR EL CALOR.
EVITA LOS HONGOS.
ELIMINA EL SALPULLIDO.

TALCO ANTISÉPTICO Z Q 9

SI NO LO CONSIGUE EN LA FARMACIA DE SU LOCALIDAD ENVIE $3.49 AL P.O. BOX 112414, SANTA FÉ, 33010 Y RECIBIRÁ UN FRASCO ORIGINAL

LA SOLUCIÓN DEL VERANO

1. What are two (2) conditions that ZQ9 is supposed to cure?
2. In what form is the medication?
3. Where is it usually available for sale?
4. If it is not where it usually is, what can the interested person do?
5. What season of the year is the need for ZQ9 most likely to occur?

Read the following carefully. DO NOT translate but answer the questions in ENGLISH.

1. What is Pajarito invited to do?
2. Who is inviting him?
3. What happens during the meetings?
4. Why is Pajarito concerned?
5. What explanation is he given?

Read the following carefully. DO NOT translate but answer the questions in ENGLISH.

Roberto está muy contento hoy porque su mamá le va a llevar a visitar a su tía en la ciudad. A Roberto le gusta mucho la casa de su tía. Es muy grande, cómoda y bonita. La tía Elena tiene muchos muebles antiguos que pertenecían a sus padres. El mecedor del bisabuelo es la pieza especial de Roberto.

Cada vez que Roberto visita a la tía Elena ella le prepara todos los postres favoritos - helados caseros, quesillo, pastel de chocolate y flan. La mamá de Roberto siempre le dice que la tía le mima demasiado porque además de darle la comida que le encanta, ella le compra ropa, y juegos para su computadora.

¡Qué tiempo maravilloso voy a tener! piensa Roberto.

1. Why is Roberto happy?
2. What does he like?
3. Why does he like it?
4. What is to be found there?
5. Who used to own these things?
6. Describe them.
7. Who owned the piece which is Roberto's favourite?
8. What happens when Roberto goes to this place?
9. What does his mother think about the situation.
10. What does Roberto think?

Read the following carefully. DO NOT translate but answer the questions in ENGLISH.

> *Rodrigo Amor y Sara M. de Amor se complacen en invitarle a usted y a su distinguida familia a la celebración del quinceañero*
>
> *de su hija*
>
> ### MARÍA DE LOS ÁNGELES
>
> *La recepción tendrá lugar el 16 de julio de 2009 de 6 p.m. a 8 p.m.: el baile de 8 p.m. a 12 medianoche en los salones del Club Campestre Los Pinos, 84 Vía de las Rosas, Pedregal de San Marcos.*

1. What is being announced?
2. Who is making the announcement?
3. Who are they?
4. Why is the announcement being made?
5. Who is María de los Ángeles?
6. In which month will the event take place?
7. What will happen between 6 - 8 p.m.?
8. What will happen at 8 p.m.?
9. Where will this take place?
10. What is the location?

Read the following carefully. DO NOT translate but answer the questions in ENGLISH.

## PEDRITO'S SURPRISE

Una tarde, mientras Pedrito regresaba de la escuela, pensaba que un día iba a ser rico. Decidió compartir su dinero con su abuelita que lo cuidaba desde que murió su mamá.

De repente vio a un hombre bajo que llevaba un sombrero grande. Pedrito, un poco miedoso, seguía caminando. Cuando estaba muy cerca del hombre, éste le dio un pequeño paquete.

Al llegar a su casa, Pedrito lo abrió y vio adentro un diamante enorme. El muchacho se dio cuenta de que el hombre era su padre que había salido hace muchos años a buscar su fortuna en el extranjero.

1.   When did the story take place?
2.   Where was Pedrito coming from?
3.   What was Pedrito thinking?
4.   What decision did he make?
5.   With whom was Pedrito living?
6.   Describe the person Pedrito saw.
7.   What did Pedrito find inside the package?
8.   What did Pedrito realise?
9.   Where had Pedrito's father gone?
10.   Why had he gone there?

Read the following carefully. DO NOT translate but answer the questions in ENGLISH.

**FLORES HOTEL & MARINA**

**El hotel más lujoso y espectacular de Isla de Perlas**

*¡Donde se hospedará la excelencia!*

- Ubicado en la Avenida San Gabriel, a orillas de la Bahía Dorada, en plena área comercial, bancaria y financiera, cerca de los centros nocturnos, teatros y demás sitios de interés turístico.
- 185 Suites y lujosas habitaciones.
- Restaurante Gourmet
- Pub
- Salones para eventos
- Exclusivo y elegante centro de negocios.
- Dos espectaculares piscinas.
- Cancha de tenis
- La más moderna Marina y Club de Yates para pesca y deportes acuáticos.

*Apertura junio de 2008*

1. In addition to a hotel, what else is Flores?
2. Where is the hotel located?
3. What is its relation to the Bahía Dorada?
4. Name two places near the hotel.
5. What is said about the rooms?
6. What eating facilities are available?
7. When did the hotel start operating?
8. What are two of the sporting events offered by the hotel?
9. Is the hotel in the city or the country?
10. Why are yachts provided?

Read the following carefully. DO NOT translate but answer the questions in ENGLISH.

## FIRE NEXT DOOR!

Una noche los miembros de la familia Roca fueron despertados por gritos que venían de la casa de los vecinos.  Los niños abrieron la ventana de su habitación y vieron a los vecinos quienes estaban acercándose a su casa. El señor Amor gritaba
   -¡Socorro! ¡Fuego!

El Señor Amor tenía sus dos hijos en los brazos.  El niño estaba llorando y gritando:
   - ¡Papí los juguetes, quiero mis juguetes!, ¡Quiero mis juguetes!
La niña gritaba:
   - ¿Dónde está mamá? ¿Dónde está mamá?
El señor Roca abrió la puerta y les dijo:
   - Pasen, pasen. ¡Dios mío! Siéntense.  Voy a llamar a los bomberos.
Raúl le dijo:  - Papá ya lo hice, y casi inmediatamente se oyó la sirena del coche de bomberos.

1.    What awoke the Roca family?
2.    What did the children do?
3.    What did they see?
4.    What was Mr. Amor shouting?
5.    Why was the boy crying?
6.    Who opened the door?
7.    What did this person do next?
8.    What did he intend to do?
9.    What did Raul tell him?
10.    What was heard?

Read the following carefully. DO NOT translate but answer the questions in ENGLISH.

El señor Roberto Mena y la señora Ana Mena
le invitan a usted y a su apreciada familia
al enlace matrimonial de su hija

CARMEN

con el señor

CARLOS MORALES LÓPEZ

hijo del señor Eduardo López y la señora
Lisa Morales de López

La ceremonia se efectuará el sábado 26 de mayo de
2009 a las cinco de la tarde en la Iglesia del Sagrado Corazón.
Se ruega pasar luego a una recepción en casa de
los padres de la novia, 234 Avenida Los Robles, Alajuela.

1. What is being sent?
2. What is the occasion?
3. When will it take place?
4. Where will it take place?
5. What event follows?
6. Where will it take place?
7. Where is this place located?
8. Who is Carmen?
9. Who is Carlos Morales López?
10. Who are Eduardo López and Lisa Morales de López?

Read the following carefully. DO NOT translate but answer the questions in ENGLISH.

---

Casa de Oro
Avenida Central
Número 2
Colombia

Querido Zacarías,

Deseo darle un cordial y amistoso saludo. Estoy muy contenta aquí en Colombia. Mi nueva amiga Carla es muy simpática y su familia es muy agradable. Su casa es muy bonita y tienen muchas fotos de diferentes partes del Caribe. He pasado dos semanas en Bogotá pero mañana vamos a Cali. La abuela de Carla vive allí y vamos a pasar una semana con ella.

Saludos a tu familia y escríbeme pronto.

Tu amiga,

María

---

1. Where is María?
2. How does she feel about being at this place?
3. Who are the persons that she has met?
4. How does she describe them?
5. What do these persons have in their house?
6. How long has María been at this place?
7. Where will she go next?
8. Who lives there?
9. How long will María spend at this place?
10. What does María want Zacarías to do?

Read the following carefully. DO NOT translate but answer the questions in ENGLISH.

**SANTA CLARA
LA ISLA HECHA
PARA SER AMADA**

UNA PORCIÓN DE TIERRA DULCE
RODEADA DE SONRISA POR
TODAS PARTES.

SANTA CLARA LE BRINDA TODO:
SU SUAVE CLIMA...
SU AIRE LIMPIO Y RENOVADOR...
SUS HERMOSAS PLAYAS
ACOGEDORAS... EL SOL
BENIGNO, SIEMPRE PRESENTE

ESTA ISLA TIENE 30
KILÓMETROS DE LARGO POR UNA
SONRISA DE ANCHO.

TIENDAS A PRECIO DE PUERTO
LIBRE.

VENGA A SANTA CLARA - LA
ISLA DE GENTE CORDIAL.
PARA TODA LA FAMILIA.

LOS ANTIGÜENSES NO NECESITAN VISA.
HAY 5 VUELOS SEMANALES.
(TWIA Y CARA).
VEA A SU AGENTE DE VIAJES.

**SANTA CLARA**
LA BELLA
DONDE LA FELICIDAD SE QUEDÓ A VIVIR.
DIRECCIÓN DE TURISMO DE SANTA CLARA, PARQUE CENTRAL
EDIFICIO HILTON (EMBAJADA DE SANTA CLARA)
PENT HOUSE - TEL. 327.04.96

1. What is given as the size of Santa Clara in the advertisement?
2. What are prices in shops like and why is this so?
3. What suggests that visitors will be happy?
4. What is said about the weather in Santa Clara?
5. What is the air like in Santa Clara?
6. In addition to being beautiful, what else is said about the beaches?
7. To what age groups is the advertisement directed?
8. How often can Antiguans go to Santa Clara?
9. Why is it easy for them to go?
10. Where can interested persons get more information?

Read the following carefully. DO NOT translate but answer the questions in ENGLISH.

# A CUALQUIER PAÍS DEL MUNDO

**LA GRAN AEROLÍNEA PALACIO**

**¡A TODOS LOS PAÍSES DEL MUNDO!**

- **Sólo Palacio le ofrece un servicio exclusivo**
- **Exquisitas comidas**
- **Finos vinos**
- **Cine en inglés y en español**
- **Música estereofónica tanto en la clase turística como en la primera clase**

**Palacio también le ofrece un programa para ganar viajes gratis a América Latina y otros destinos internacionales.**

**Vuela con Palacio siempre.**
**Es seguro.**
**No olvidará el vuelo nunca.**
**Llámanos ahora a nuestra oficina: 555-212-345**

**PALACIO**

**Las alas del Mundo**

1. What is being advertised?
2. What is its name?
3. Name two things which are offered.
4. What is offered in two languages?
5. What entertainment is available?
6. What is offered in both classes?
7. What special programme is also being offered?
8. Why should people use this service?
9. What will people never forget?
10. What are people asked to do immediately?

Read the following carefully. DO NOT translate but answer the questions in ENGLISH.

---

## VENDA MA$

**MOTIVE Y ORGANICE A SUS VENDEDORES**

**SEMINARIO**

**"VENTAS MI PROFESIÓN"**

¡Con 15 años de experiencia
capacitando Vendedores!

**Temas**
* Factores para triunfar en Ventas.
* Planes de acción y objetivos.
* Organización del tiempo y reportes

| LUGAR: Hotel del Bosque - Melchor Ocampo 323, México, DF 03100 |
| DÍA: 23 de febrero de 8:30 A.M. a 6:30 P.M. |
| COSTO: N$ 600 + I.V.A |

*INSCRIPCIONES:* Avenida Pesado No. 110-1c Col. Del Valle, México, D.F. 03100

**Tel./Fax 523-7632  687-1550  682-9851  669-1828**

---

1. To whom is the advertisement directed?
2. What is this person encouraged to do?
3. What is being advertised?
4. Where will the event take place?
5. What does the person advertising say about himself?
6. What are two topics which will be dealt with during the event?
7. What is the cost of attending the event?
8. What can be achieved by attending?
9. How can the advertiser be contacted?
10. How long will the event last?

Read the following carefully. DO NOT translate but answer the questions in ENGLISH.

**AVENTURAS DE NAVEGACIÓN**

Puede descubrir las maravillas de la navegación en estilo y comodidad a bordo de uno de nuestros barcos de lujo.

**CRUCERO DE MAGNOLIS LE OFRECE**

**CRUCEROS MÁGICOS A DOSCIENTOS DESTINOS DIFERENTES.**

Ofrecemos durante todo el año:

- Precios bajos
- Personales agradables
- Una experiencia inolvidable.

Esperamos su llamada a nuestra oficina.     888-559-222
O si prefiere, visítenos.  Estamos a la orden.

Calle Quinto, Número 8.

1. What does this advertisement offer?
2. How will passengers travel?
3. How are the ships described ?
4. What is the name of the company which placed this advertisement?
5. What is being advertised?
6. How many different places are mentioned in the offer?
7. Name two things the company offers.
8. When is the offer available?
9. Where is the company located?
10. How can one obtain further information?

Read the following carefully. DO NOT translate but answer the questions in ENGLISH.

La vida en la región donde vivía el Hermano Anansi era muy difícil. No llovía y las plantas, la tierra y toda la vegetación estaban secas. No había nada como alimento para los animales que sufrían de hambre. Un día el Hermano Anansi y el Hermano Perro se dieron cuenta de que había un maizal al otro lado del río. El Hermano Perro se ofreció a llevar a Anansi en la espalda al otro lado del río. Al llegar al maizal Anansi y el Hermano Perro seleccionaron los mejores mazorcas de maíz. Pero Anansi no quería compartir el maíz con el Hermano Perro. Cuando el Hermano Perro empezó a comer el maíz, el Hermano Anansi empezó a gritar para llamar la atención del dueño del maizal.

Cuando el amo oyó los gritos de Anansi corrió al maizal con un palo grueso que usó para golpear al Hermano Perro mientras el Hermano Anansi se escondió. Cuando el dueño salió con el pobre Hermano Perro como prisionero, Anansi se quedó en la granja y todos los días comía el maíz con alegría.

1. Describe the area in which Anansi lived.
2. Why was it like this?
3. What problem did this situation create?
4. What did Anansi discover?
5. Who discovered this with him ?
6. How did Hermano Anansi get across the river?
7. What did they do when they got there?
8. What did Anansi do afterwards?
9. Why did he do this?
10. What happened to Hermano Perro?

Read the following carefully. DO NOT translate but answer the questions in ENGLISH.

# GRAN JEFE

## SU VIAJE A PAULINA EN PRIMERA CLASE

De Puerto Verde a San Pedro en sólo dos horas. Sin colas y sin pérdidas de tiempo. Disfrute del más lujoso y confortable viaje en la exclusiva flota Gran Jefe, que ahora cuenta con tres unidades.

Gran Jefe, un estupendo viaje en auténtica primera clase, con televisión a color y la fabulosa atención de nuestras atractivas y simpáticas nautimozas.

**Puerto Verde**
Hotel Melía, Local 3
Principal
Teléfono: (081) 24.241
Terminal MOCARA
Final Av. Principal del Paraíso

**Punta de Salima**
Terminal Muelle

Teléfono: (095) 98.128

**San Juan**
Calle Marcano, a una cuadra de la Plaza Central
Teléfono: (095) 23.461

**TURISMO SAN PEDRO C.A. LA EMPRESA GRANDE DE ORIENTE**

1. Where does the trip start?
2. How long is the trip?
3. Where is the company which placed the advertisment located?
4. What will the traveller be saved?
5. What is authentic about this trip?
6. Who attends to passengers?
7. What is said about them?
8. What is provided to entertain passengers?
9. Where is the port located in San Juan?
10. How many boats does the company have?

116

Read the following carefully. DO NOT translate but answer the questions in ENGLISH.

**NUEVA OFICINA DEL BANCO OPINIÓN**
**2000 AVENIDA CENTRAL**

*OFRECE TODOS LOS SERVICIOS BANCARIOS*
A LOS CLIENTES DEL BANCO OPINIÓN
Las puertas se abrirán el 10 de agosto de **2009**

- Cuentas corrientes
- Cuentas de ahorro
- Transferencias
- Certificados de Depósitos y mucho más.
- Impuestos bajos

Para Información Adicional, Favor llamar:  **552 7711**

*BANCO OPINIÓN - EL BANCO DE CONFIANZA*

1. What is being advertised?
2. What is the name of the company which placed this advertisement?
3. When will these services become available?
4. What are low in this company?
5. What kind of services does this company provide?
6. Name two of these services.
7. Where is this company located?
8. Why is the number 552 7711 included?
9. How is the company described?
10. How do we know that the company offers other services besides the
    ones specified?

Read the following carefully. DO NOT translate but answer the questions in ENGLISH.

**Altaña Tennis Club**

La Junta Directiva y Socios del Altaña Tennis Club,
cumplen con el penoso deber de participar el sensible
fallecimiento de la señora

*Paloma Salazar*
*(Q.E.P.D.)*

Madre de nuestro consocio Ricardo Salazar, a quien
hacemos llegar nuestras más sentidas expresiones de
condolencia, extensiva a su esposa e hijos, demás
familiares y amigos.

Caracas, 9 de diciembre de 2008.

1. Who placed this announcement?
2. What are they expressing?
3. What is their connection with Ricardo Salazar?
4. Who is Paloma Salazar?
5. What has happened to her?
6. What obligation are the two groups fulfilling?
7. Why is this obligation considered 'penoso'?
8. What is the meaning of Q.E.P.D.?
9. Who are the main persons to whom the announcement is directed?
10. Who else is referred to?

118

Read the following carefully. DO NOT translate but answer the questions in ENGLISH.

**Hasta
un hombre
invisible
necesita
estar
cubierto**

¡Cúbrase por
completo!

A pesar de sus extraños poderes,
un hombre invisible sabe que él también
puede sufrir un accidente:
su transparencia no es más que una
forma de protección.
Así como un hombre invisible trata de estar
cubierto, asimismo usted y su familia
necesitan sentirse seguros.
Un seguro de Vida y una póliza Contra Accidentes
son la mejor manera de demostrar todo
el amor que usted siente por los suyos.  Consulte con su
Productor y él le dirá por qué
SEGUROS ÁGUILA es cobertura segura.
Hasta los superhéroes necesitan estar cubiertos...
cúbrase usted también con SEGUROS ÁGUILA.
**Siéntase Superseguro Y Cúbrase Por
Completo Con**

# SEGUROS ÁGUILA

1. What is the name of the company that has placed this advertisement?
2. What is the business of this company?
3. What is the invisible man said to have?
4. What could happen to the invisible man?
5. Why is being invisible not enough?
6. What are the two types of protection the company is offering?
7. What is a good way of showing love for your family?
8. What is said about superheroes?
9. To whom is the advertisement directed?
10. How will you feel if you take the advice in the advertisement?

Read the following carefully. DO NOT translate but answer the questions in ENGLISH.

## PREPARING TO MAKE "AREBA"

Una actividad importante en la vida de los garífunas es la preparación del pan de yuca. Este pan seco llamado "areba" se prepara con la raíz de la yuca, una planta que se cultiva en los trópicos como alimento y es un legado de los indios caribes.

La preparación del pan es un largo proceso que comienza con la cosecha de las raíces de la yuca. Por lo general, las mujeres y los niños se levantan antes del amanecer y se dirigen a las granjas que en Belice están situadas en medio de la selva, entre ocho y quince kilómetros de los pueblos. A la sombra de las palmas, recogen de dieciocho a veinte kilógramos de raíces de yuca. Cuando terminan, llevan la yuca en canastas sobre la cabeza hasta la aldea.

Al llegar a las aldeas, para protegerse del sol van debajo de las casas que son construídas sobre postes. Allí las mujeres y los niños pelan y lavan las raíces. Después las rallan sobre planchas de madera con piedras agudas. Las mujeres acompañan el trabajo con canciones en que hablan de la tristeza y de la vida en general.

1.  What is "Areba"
2.  What do the garífunas use to prepare it?
3.  Where is this grown and for what purpose?
4.  How does the process of preparing "areba" begin?
5.  Who are involved in this process?
6.  Approximately how much of the crop is reaped?
7.  Where are the farms usually located in Belize?
8.  Why do the women and children go under the house?
9.  What two things do they do there first?
10. What do the women do as they work?

Read the following carefully. DO NOT translate but answer the questions in ENGLISH.

| 41742 | | | | | |
|---|---|---|---|---|---|
| **ESTADO DE CUENTA** | HABIT No. 712 | NOMBRE *Felipe González Amor* 1/488000 | | | PERS./TARIFA |
| **Hotel CONTINENTAL** ☆☆☆☆☆☆ Guayaquil - Ecuador | RECEPCIONISTA | SALIDA 29 de nov. de 2008 | | LLEGADA 21 de nov. de 2008 | |
| Chile y 10 de Agosto Esquina Tel: 329270 Casilla-09-01-4510 Telefax: 04-325454 | | OBSERVACIONES | | | |

| | FECHA | CONCEPTO | CARGOS | ABONOS | SALDO | SALDO ANTERIOR |
|---|---|---|---|---|---|---|
| 1 | NOV.22.08 | COMU 712 | *2,800.00 | | *2,889.00 | ***2,880.00 |
| 2 | NOV.22.08 | HABIT 712 | 488,000.00 | | | |
| 3 | NOV.22.08 | SERVC 712 | *48,800.00 | | | |
| 4 | NOV.22.08 | IMPTO 712 | *48,800.00 | | 588,480.00* | *588,480.00 |
| 5 | NOV.23.08 | COMU 712 | 28,800.00 | | 617,280.00 | *617,280.00 |
| 6 | NOV.23.08 | CAJA 712 | | 617,280.00 | * .00 | |
| 7 | NOV.25.08 | LAVAN | 30,000.00 | | | |
| 8 | NOV.26.08 | CAFETERIA | 22,000.00 | | | |
| 9 | | | | | | |
| 10 | | | | | | |
| 11 | | | | | | |
| 12 | | | | | | |

SÍMBOLOS:        REG. UNIC. No. 0990000085001

| HABIT: | HABITACIÓN | R.SERV: | SERVICIO HABITAC | FIRMA DEL HUESPED |
|---|---|---|---|---|
| PENS. | PENSIÓN | COMUN: | COMUNICACIONES | *J. González* |
| SERV: | SERVICIO | LAVAN: | LAVANDERÍA | |
| IMPTO: | IMPUESTO | VARS: | VARIOS | |
| CAFET: | CAFETERÍA | DESE: | DESEMBOLSOS | DIRECCIÓN: *Apartado 10. Calle Madrid* |
| C-BAR: | COMEDOR BAR | PROP: | PROPINAS | |
| DESC: | DESCUENTO | | | APROBADO POR: *Raúl López Mena* |

1.     What is being shown?
2.     Which place has prepared this document and for whom?
3.     What is the address of this place?
4.     When did this person arrive there?
5.     Where did he/she occupy?
6.     How much was charged for tax?
7.     Why was 2,800.00 sucres recorded on November 22?
8.     How much was spent in the cafeteria on November 26?
9.     On what was 30,000 sucres spent on November 25?
10.    What was the cost of the place where the person stayed?

Read the following carefully. DO NOT translate but answer the questions in ENGLISH.

---

BANCO DEL PACÍFICO _____ 08/11/23
Fecha
No. 1117090

## COMPROBANTE DE NEGOCIACIÓN DE DIVISAS

Nombre del Cliente: _____ *Michael Ramsay* _____

C.I/R.U.C./Pasaporte No. _____ 211100432 _____

Dirección __ *7 Carnation Path, Kingston 7, Jamaica* __ Teléfono _____ 809-92-77777 _____

### TIPO DE TRANSACCIÓN

Compra ☐          Venta ☑

Billete ☐          Cheque ☐          Otros ☐

| Moneda | Valor en Moneda Extranjera US$40 | Tipo de Cambio 6273 | Valor en Moneda Nacional 250.QW |
|---|---|---|---|

### INSTRUCCIONES DEL CLIENTE

☐ Débito a Cuenta:                    ☐ Crédito a Cuenta:

Tipo ____ No. _____          Tipo ____ No. __ *412018-9 Sucres*

Tipo ____ No. _____          Tipo ____ No. _____

☐ Efectivo _____            ☐ Cheque _____

Observaciones _____

Tipo: A=Ahorros          C=Corriente          D=Dólares

Autorizo a efectuar la transacción en Divisas de acuerdo a instruciones.

Declaro que los fondos de esta operación bancaria tienen origen o destino lícito.

*M. Ramsay*

_____          _____
Elaborado por                    Firma del Cliente

1. What is being shown?
2. Who did the transaction?
3. What does the number 211100432 represent?
4. In which country does the person reside?
5. What kind of transaction did he do?
6. What does 6273 represent?
7. What did the person receive?
8. What does the person declare when he signs?

Read the following carefully.   DO NOT translate but answer the questions in ENGLISH.

## ZONA

**REPÚBLICA DE PANAMÁ**
**DEPARTMENTO DE MIGRACIÓN**
**TARJETA INTERNACIONAL DE EMBARQUE/DESEMBARQUE**

Título

Sr.       Srta. ☑

Sra.      Otro ☐

FAVOR USAR LETRA DE MOLDE      Sexo   M ☐   F ☑

NOMBRE COMPLETO

| R | A | M | Í | R | E | Z | | L | Ó | P | E | Z |
|---|---|---|---|---|---|---|---|---|---|---|---|---|

Apellidos

| Á | N | G | E | L | A | | M | A | R | Í | A |
|---|---|---|---|---|---|---|---|---|---|---|---|

Nombres

PAÍS DE NACIMIENTO _____ Costa Rica   Edad   22

NACIONALIDAD: _____ Costarricense _____ OCUPACIÓN: _____ Periodista

NÚMERO DE FAMILIARES QUE VIAJA CON Vd. _____

DOMICILIO PERMANENTE: _____ San José _____ Heredia _____ Costa Rica
                             Ciudad              Prov. O Estado        País

DIRECCIÓN POSTAL: _____ Apartado 1346, Escazú, San José

PASAPORTE No. _____ 2234560 _____ LUGAR DE EXPEDICIÓN: _____ San José ~ Costa Rica

MOTIVO DE VIAJE      RECREO ☐      NEGOCIOS ☐

     CONVENCIONES ☑      OTROS _____ Posibilidad de Obtener Empleo
                                                    Específique

TIEMPO DE ESTADÍA EN PANAMÁ: _____ Siete _____ DÍAS

PUERTO DE EMBARQUE: _____ San José, Costa Rica

DOMICILIO EN PANAMA: _____ Hotel Solar

---

INFORMACIÓN DE SALIDA (Adicional)

PAÍS Y CIUDAD DE DESTINO: _____

TIEMPO DE ESTADÍA EN ESE LUGAR: _____

COMPAÑÍA _____ VUELO No. _____

PAZ Y SALVO No. _____

---

1. What type of form is being shown?
2. Which agency issued this form?
3. What is the full name of the person who is completing the form?
4. In which country was the person born?
5. What is the person's profession?
6. How many other family members are travelling with the person?
7. Where does the person live in his/her country?
8. State two reasons why the person is travelling to Panama.
9. How long will the person be in Panama?
10. Where does the person intend to stay in Panama?

125

Read the following carefully.  DO NOT translate but answer the questions in ENGLISH.

Cuéntanos tu historia
de amor
y viaja gratis
a
Sudamérica

Casa de Lujo, uno de los complejos turísticos más lujosos del Ecuador, te recibirá durante una semana, si nos cuentas tu mejor historia de amor.

Seguro que tienes alguna anécdota romántica o divertida del momento en que miraste por primera vez a tu novio o novia.  Queremos que todos nuestros lectores que están planificando la boda nos escriban. El punto de vista masculino nos interesa muchísimo.

Entre todas las cartas recibidas, con las mejores historias de amor se sorteará un viaje PARA DOS PERSONAS A CASA DE LUJO. ¡Participa y haz un viaje de sueño a Sudamérica.  Esperamos tus cartas hasta el 20 de junio.

Casa de Lujo
P.O. Box 149
Quito, Ecuador

1.  What is this advertisement inviting readers to do?
2.  Which company has placed this advertisement?
3.  Which readers is this advertisement targeting?
4.  What kind of company is it?
5.  What kinds of stories do they want their readers to share?
6.  What is of particular interest to them?
7.  What will the writer/writers of the best story receive?
8.  What will happen on June 20?

Read the following carefully. DO NOT translate but answer the questions in ENGLISH.

**PUEDE SER TUYO**

¡UN TRAJE DE BODA FABULOSO!

Dimitrio Gambril es el diseñador de trajes de novia preferido por la alta sociedad. Las novias elegantes y sofisticadas se casan en sus vestidos espectaculares. Tienen ricos bordados y cortes precisos que acentúan la ligereza del talle. Hay diseños modernos con damascos y brocados; hay diseños suntuosos para dar el sí el día más feliz de tu vida. Uno de estos vestidos espléndidos puede ser tuyo, hecho a medida, a un precio bajo. Es un regalo para la novia elegante que no tiene mucho dinero. Una oferta increíble.

¡Llámenos a nuestro salón!

Dimitrio Gambril
Avenida Sur
28006 Santiago, Chile
43505 00.

1. What is being advertised?
2. Who is Dimitrio Gambril?
3. What is special about this product?
4. What two types of materials are named?
5. How are these products made?
6. Who is being offered this product at a low price?
7. What should interested persons do?
8. In which part of the country is the designer located?